I0411777

A successful marriage requires falling in love many times, always with the same person.

Mignon McLaughlin

Happy is the man who finds a true friend, and far happier is he who finds that true friend in his wife.

Franz Schubert

My husband and I are best of friends first and foremost. We fight like cats and dogs, but never stay mad for long. I was lucky to find him, he is in every way, my soulmate.

Carnie Wilson

By all means, marry. If you get a good wife, you'll become happy; if you get a bad one, you'll become a philosopher.

Socrates

The secret to a happy marriage is if you can be at peace with someone within four walls, if you are content because the one you love is near to you, either upstairs or downstairs, or in the same room, and you feel that warmth that you don't find very often, then that is what love is all about.

Bruce Forsyth

My most brilliant achievement was my ability to be able to persuade my wife to marry me.

Winston Churchill

Marriage is neither heaven nor hell, it is simply purgatory.

Abraham Lincoln

When marrying, ask yourself this question: Do you believe that you will be able to converse well with this person into your old age? Everything else in marriage is transitory.

Friedrich Nietzsche

I love being married. It's so great to find that one special person you want to annoy for the rest of your life.

Rita Rudner

Don't marry the person you think you can live with; marry only the individual you think you can't live without.

James Dobson

It is not a lack of love, but a lack of friendship that makes unhappy marriages.

Friedrich Nietzsche

All married couples should learn the art of battle as they should learn the art of making love. Good battle is objective and honest - never vicious or cruel. Good battle is healthy and constructive, and brings to a marriage the principles of equal partnership.

Ann Landers

A good husband makes a good wife.

John Florio

To keep your marriage brimming, With love in the loving cup, Whenever you're wrong, admit it; Whenever you're right, shut up.

Ogden Nash

It is a full time job being honest one moment at a time, remembering to love, to honor, to respect. It is a practice, a discipline, worthy of every moment.

Jasmine Guy

A good marriage would be between a blind wife and a deaf husband.

Michel de Montaigne

In a happy marriage it is the wife who provides the climate, the husband the landscape.

Gerald Brenan

In marriage there are no manners to keep up, and beneath the wildest accusations no real criticism. Each is familiar with that ancient child in the other who may erupt again. We are not ridiculous to ourselves. We are ageless. That is the luxury of the wedding ring.

Enid Bagnold

I have learned that only two things are necessary to keep one's wife happy. First, let her think she's having her own way. And second, let her have it.

Lyndon B. Johnson

Let the wife make the husband glad to come home, and let

him make her sorry to see him leave.

Martin Luther

There is nothing nobler or more admirable than when two people who see eye to eye keep house as man and wife, confounding their enemies and delighting their friends.

Homer

There is nothing in the world like the devotion of a married woman. It is a thing no married man knows anything about.

Oscar Wilde

Every good relationship, especially marriage, is based on respect. If it's not based on respect, nothing that appears to be good will last very long.

Amy Grant

But marriage goes in waves. You've got to be patient. People bail and give up on their marriages way too early. They just don't put the work and the effort into it. You've got to suck up your ego a lot of times, because that can be a big downfall.

Anna Benson

When you make the sacrifice in marriage, you're sacrificing not to each other but to unity in a relationship.

Joseph Campbell

On rare occasions one does hear of a miraculous case of a married couple falling in love after marriage, but on close examination it will be found that it is a mere adjustment to the inevitable.

Emma Goldman

Marriage is an adventure, like going to war.

Gilbert K. Chesterton

Do you know what it means to come home at night to a woman who'll give you a little love, a little affection, a little tenderness? It means you're in the wrong house, that's what it means.

Henny Youngman

The secret of a happy marriage remains a secret.

Henny Youngman

A happy marriage is a long conversation which always seems too short.

Andre Maurois

Marriage is like a cage; one sees the birds outside desperate to get in, and those inside equally desperate to get out.

Michel de Montaigne

Before marriage, a girl has to make love to a man to hold him. After marriage, she has to hold him to make love to him.

Marilyn Monroe

Sensual pleasures have the fleeting brilliance of a comet; a happy marriage has the tranquillity of a lovely sunset.

Ann Landers

For years my wedding ring has done its job. It has led me not into temptation. It has reminded my husband numerous times at parties that it's time to go home. It has been a source of relief to a dinner companion. It has been a status symbol in the maternity ward.

Erma Bombeck

All men make mistakes, but married men find out about them sooner.

Red Skelton

Marriages are made in heaven and consummated on Earth.

John Lyly

Marriage is a wonderful invention: then again, so is a bicycle repair kit.

Billy Connolly

One advantage of marriage is that, when you fall out of love with him or he falls out of love with you, it keeps you together until you fall in again.

Judith Viorst

Marriage has made me a lot happier and I'm deeply in love with my wife, and I thank God for her every day.

Harry Connick, Jr.

If you want to know how your girl will treat you after marriage, just listen to her talking to her little brother.

Sam Levenson

Basically my wife was immature. I'd be at home in the bath and she'd come in and sink my boats.

Woody Allen

It is a truth universally acknowledged, that a single man in possession of a good fortune, must be in want of a wife.

Jane Austen

Keep your eyes wide open before marriage, half shut afterwards.

Benjamin Franklin

If there is such a thing as a good marriage, it is because it resembles friendship rather than love.

Michel de Montaigne

My wife is my soul mate. I can't imagine being without her.

Matt Damon

The difficulty with marriage is that we fall in love with a personality, but must live with a character.

Peter De Vries

It's tough to stay married. My wife kisses the dog on the lips, yet she won't drink from my glass.

Rodney Dangerfield

I think the best thing I can do is to be a distraction. A husband lives and breathes his work all day long. If he comes home to more table thumping, how can the poor man ever relax?

Jackie Kennedy

By our Heavenly Father and only because of God, only because of God. We're like other couples. We do not get along perfectly; we do not go without arguments and, as I call them, fights, and heartache and pain and hurting each other. But a marriage is three of us.

Barbara Mandrell

Getting divorced just because you don't love a man is almost as silly as getting married just because you do.

Zsa Zsa Gabor

There's only one way to have a happy marriage and as soon as I learn what it is I'll get married again.

Clint Eastwood

A man in love is incomplete until he has married. Then he's finished.

Zsa Zsa Gabor

Happiness in marriage is entirely a matter of chance.

Jane Austen

Marriage has no guarantees. If that's what you're looking for, go live with a car battery.

Erma Bombeck

Never get married in college; it's hard to get a start if a prospective employer finds you've already made one mistake.

Elbert Hubbard

When a man opens a car door for his wife, it's either a new car or a new wife.

Prince Philip

Marriage is the highest state of friendship. If happy, it lessens our cares by dividing them, at the same time that it doubles our pleasures by mutual participation.

Samuel Richardson

Men have a much better time of it than women. For one thing, they marry later; for another thing, they die earlier.

H. L. Mencken

Married men live longer than single men. But married men are a lot more willing to die.

Johnny Carson

A successful marriage is an edifice that must be rebuilt every day.

Andre Maurois

One should always be in love. That is the reason one should never marry.

Oscar Wilde

A good husband is never the first to go to sleep at night or the last to awake in the morning.

Honore de Balzac

Marriage is not about age; it's about finding the right person.

Sophia Bush

Like everything which is not the involuntary result of fleeting emotion but the creation of time and will, any marriage, happy or unhappy, is infinitely more interesting than any romance, however passionate.

W. H. Auden

A journey is like marriage. The certain way to be wrong is to think you control it.

John Steinbeck

Marriage is good for those who are afraid to sleep alone at night.

St. Jerome

Marriage is a wonderful institution, but who wants to live in an institution?

Groucho Marx

Marriage is nature's way of keeping us from fighting with strangers.

Alan King

Marriage is an attempt to solve problems together which you didn't even have when you were on your own.

Eddie Cantor

The first time you marry for love, the second for money, and the third for companionship.

Jackie Kennedy

Men who have a pierced ear are better prepared for marriage - they've experienced pain and bought jewelry.

Rita Rudner

I'd marry again if I found a man who had fifteen million dollars, would sign over half to me, and guarantee that he'd be dead within a year.

Bette Davis

Well married a person has wings, poorly married shackles.

Henry Ward Beecher

Marriage is a great institution, but I'm not ready for an institution.

Mae West

Love: A temporary insanity curable by marriage.

Ambrose Bierce

There were three of us in this marriage, so it was a bit crowded.

Princess Diana

An ideal wife is any woman who has an ideal husband.

Booth Tarkington

Marriage should be a duet - when one sings, the other claps.

Joe Murray

Always get married in the morning. That way if it doesn't work out, you haven't wasted the whole day.

Mickey Rooney

The majority of husbands remind me of an orangutan trying to play the violin.

Honore de Balzac

Marriage: A word which should be pronounced 'mirage'.

Herbert Spencer

For marriage to be a success, every woman and every man
should have her and his own bathroom. The end.

Catherine Zeta-Jones

Bachelors have consciences, married men have wives.

Samuel Johnson

When a man steals your wife, there is no better revenge
than to let him keep her.

Sacha Guitry

Marriage resembles a pair of shears, so joined that they
cannot be separated; often moving in opposite directions,
yet always punishing anyone who comes between them.

Sydney Smith

If you made a list of reasons why any couple got married,
and another list of the reasons for their divorce, you'd have
a hell of a lot of overlapping.

Mignon McLaughlin

All that a husband or wife really wants is to be pitied a little, praised a little, and appreciated a little.

Oliver Goldsmith

When you have a baby, love is automatic, when you get married, love is earned.

Marie Osmond

Marriage is the alliance of two people, one of whom never remembers birthdays and the other who never forgets them.

Ogden Nash

Let us now set forth one of the fundamental truths about marriage: the wife is in charge.

Bill Cosby

Marriage must incessantly contend with a monster that devours everything: familiarity.

Honore de Balzac

Take care of him. And make him feel important. And if you can do that, you'll have a happy and wonderful marriage. Like two out of every ten couples.

Neil Simon

Marrying a man is like buying something you've been admiring for a long time in a shop window. You may love it when you get it home, but it doesn't always go with everything else in the house.

Jean Kerr

I think women are natural caretakers. They take care of everybody. They take care of their husbands and their kids and their dogs, and don't spend a lot of time just getting back and taking time out.

Reese Witherspoon

Any intelligent woman who reads the marriage contract, and then goes into it, deserves all the consequences.

Isadora Duncan

Marriage is a bribe to make the housekeeper think she's a

householder.

Thornton Wilder

Many a man in love with a dimple makes the mistake of marrying the whole girl.

Stephen Leacock

If I get married, I want to be very married.

Audrey Hepburn

If you want to sacrifice the admiration of many men for the criticism of one, go ahead, get married.

Katharine Hepburn

She's been married so many times she has rice marks on her face.

Henny Youngman

Only choose in marriage a man whom you would choose as a friend if he were a woman.

Joseph Joubert

Bachelors know more about women than married men; if they didn't they'd be married too.

H. L. Mencken

Love is moral even without legal marriage, but marriage is immoral without love.

Ellen Key

All marriages are happy. It's the living together afterward that causes all the trouble.

Raymond Hull

I married the first man I ever kissed. When I tell this to my children, they just about throw up.

Barbara Bush

Instead of getting married again, I'm going to find a woman I don't like and give her a house.

Lewis Grizzard

Faithful women are all alike, they think only of their fidelity, never of their husbands.

Jean Giraudoux

When I get married, it'll be no secret.

Elvis Presley

A so-called happy marriage corresponds to love as a correct poem to an improvised song.

Karl Wilhelm Friedrich Schlegel

Here in Hollywood you can actually get a marriage license printed on an Etch-A-Sketch.

Dennis Miller

He's the kind of man a woman would have to marry to get rid of.

Mae West

It's not beauty but fine qualities, my girl, that keep a husband.

Euripides

Marrying for love may be a bit risky, but it is so honest
that God can't help but smile on it.

Josh Billings

Marriage, n: the state or condition of a community
consisting of a master, a mistress, and two slaves, making
in all, two.

Ambrose Bierce

Love is often the fruit of marriage.

Moliere

A psychiatrist asks a lot of expensive questions your wife
asks for nothing.

Joey Adams

No man is regular in his attendance at the House of
Commons until he is married.

Benjamin Disraeli

A wedding is a funeral where you smell your own flowers.

Eddie Cantor

I've had an exciting time; I married for love and got a little money along with it.

Rose Kennedy

Never feel remorse for what you have thought about your wife; she has thought much worse things about you.

Jean Rostand

Marriage, it seems, confines every man to his proper rank.

Jean de la Bruyere

Love in marriage should be the accomplishment of a beautiful dream, and not, as it too often is, the end.

Alphonse Karr

Marriage is a difficult project. When seven years have passed and all your body's cells have been replaced, you're meant to experience that seven-year itch.

Yoko Ono

When a marriage works, nothing on earth can take its place.

Helen Gahagan

Whoever, fleeing marriage and the sorrows that women cause, does not wish to wed comes to a deadly old age.

Hesiod

The critical period of matrimony is breakfast-time.

A. P. Herbert

Marriage - a book of which the first chapter is written in poetry and the remaining chapters in prose.

Beverley Nichols

Where there's marriage without love, there will be love without marriage.

Benjamin Franklin

Marrying an old bachelor is like buying second-hand furniture.

H. Jackson Brown, Jr.

Politics doesn't make strange bedfellows - marriage does.

Groucho Marx

Husbands are like fires - they go out when they're left unattended.

Cher

Marriage is a series of desperate arguments people feel passionately about.

Katharine Hepburn

Marriage may be the closest thing to Heaven or Hell any of us will know on this earth.

Edwin Louis Cole

An ideal wife is one who remains faithful to you but tries

to be just as charming as if she weren't.

Sacha Guitry

Marriage is a great institution.

Elizabeth Taylor

A husband is what is left of a lover, after the nerve has been extracted.

Helen Rowland

It isn't tying himself to one woman that a man dreads when he thinks of marrying; it's separating himself from all the others.

Helen Rowland

In Hollywood a marriage is a success if it outlasts milk.

Rita Rudner

I don't think my wife likes me very much, when I had a heart attack she wrote for an ambulance.

Frank Carson

They dream in courtship, but in wedlock wake.

Alexander Pope

In olden times sacrifices were made at the altar - a practice which is still continued.

Helen Rowland

Marriage is a feast where the grace is sometimes better than the dinner.

Charles Caleb Colton

Marriage is a gamble, let's be honest.

Yoko Ono

He that loves not his wife and children feeds a lioness at home, and broods a nest of sorrows.

Jeremy Taylor

I enjoy being single, but I loved being married.

Stephanie Mills

Daddy was real gentle with kids. That's why I expected so much out of marriage, figuring that all men should be steady and pleasant.

Loretta Lynn

I like getting married, but I don't like being married.

Don Adams

If you want to read about love and marriage, you've got to buy two separate books.

Alan King

Bring a wife home to your house when you are of the right age, not far short of 30 years, nor much above; this is the right time for marriage.

Hesiod

Protecting the institution of marriage safeguards, I believe, the American family.

John Boehner

It's not always been a happy marriage. I guess I wanted a quick fix.

David Byrne

I married beneath me, all women do.

Nancy Astor

One was never married, and that's his hell; another is, and that's his plague.

Robert Burton

The only good husbands stay bachelors: They're too considerate to get married.

Finley Peter Dunne

Marriage, like money, is still with us; and, like money, progressively devalued.

Robert Graves

Marriage is a mistake every man should make.

George Jessel

I think it's something that needs to be said - that there are interracial marriages out there, and the couples live happy lives, and there's nothing wrong with it.

Tia Mowry

I might be celibate, but I appreciate the wonder of the sacrament of marriage.

Keith O'Brien

Marriage is an exercise in torture.

Frances Conroy

But to sustain a marriage for 50 years, you have to get real a little bit and find someone who is understanding and who you can grow with. My mom always says, 'Marry the man who loves you a millimeter more.'

Ali Larter

I very much feel that marriage is a sacrament and that sacrament should extend... to that legal entity of a union between what traditionally in our Western values has been defined as between a man and a woman.

Bill Frist

Marriage, for a woman at least, hampers the two things that made life to me glorious - friendship and learning.

Jane Harrison

I wanted to marry a girl just like my mom.

Michael Bergin

Marriage is a financial contract; I have enough contracts already.

Linda Fiorentino

The comfortable estate of widowhood is the only hope that keeps up a wife's spirits.

John Gay

Experts on romance say for a happy marriage there has to be more than a passionate love. For a lasting union, they insist, there must be a genuine liking for each other. Which, in my book, is a good definition for friendship.

Marilyn Monroe

The real act of marriage takes place in the heart, not in the ballroom or church or synagogue. It's a choice you make - not just on your wedding day, but over and over again - and that choice is reflected in the way you treat your husband or wife.

Barbara de Angelis

I believe marriage is between a man and a woman. I am not in favor of gay marriage. But when you start playing around with constitutions, just to prohibit somebody who cares about another person, it just seems to me that's not what America's about. Usually, our constitutions expand liberties, they don't contract them.

Barack Obama

There is no more lovely, friendly and charming relationship, communion or company than a good marriage.

Martin Luther

Chains do not hold a marriage together. It is threads, hundreds of tiny threads, which sew people together through the years.

Simone Signoret

The secret of a happy marriage is finding the right person. You know they're right if you love to be with them all the time.

Julia Child

So many people prefer to live in drama because it's comfortable. It's like someone staying in a bad marriage or relationship - it's actually easier to stay because they know what to expect every day, versus leaving and not knowing what to expect.

Ellen DeGeneres

The heart of marriage is memories; and if the two of you happen to have the same ones and can savor your reruns, then your marriage is a gift from the gods.

Bill Cosby

Getting married, for me, was the best thing I ever did. I was suddenly beset with an immense sense of release, that we have something more important than our separate selves, and that is the marriage. There's immense happiness that can come from working towards that.

Nick Cave

Some people ask the secret of our long marriage. We take time to go to a restaurant two times a week. A little candlelight, dinner, soft music and dancing. She goes Tuesdays, I go Fridays.

Henny Youngman

Marriage is an act of will that signifies and involves a mutual gift, which unites the spouses and binds them to their eventual souls, with whom they make up a sole family - a domestic church.

Pope John Paul II

After about 20 years of marriage, I'm finally starting to scratch the surface of what women want. And I think the answer lies somewhere between conversation and chocolate.

Mel Gibson

In terms of my marriage, you know, falling in love with my husband was by far the best thing that's ever happened to me.

Caroline Kennedy

Romantic love is an illusion. Most of us discover this truth at the end of a love affair or else when the sweet emotions of love lead us into marriage and then turn down their flames.

Thomas Moore

I have yet to hear a man ask for advice on how to combine marriage and a career.

Gloria Steinem

My thoughts on gay marriage are that everyone has the right to love and be loved, and that's the position I take.

Nick Jonas

Marriage is an alliance entered into by a man who can't sleep with the window shut, and a woman who can't sleep with the window open.

George Bernard Shaw

In my divorce, I stood up and said to my ex-wife, 'Hey, I messed up. This had nothing to do with you. I didn't understand what marriage was. I cheated. I was wrong. We couldn't fix it; it got worse. I stepped away because I didn't want it to get any worse. You're the mother of my kids - I don't want to hate you.'

Kevin Hart

Crucial to understanding federalism in modern day America is the concept of mobility, or 'the ability to vote with your feet.' If you don't support the death penalty and citizens packing a pistol - don't come to Texas. If you don't like medicinal marijuana and gay marriage, don't move to California.

Rick Perry

Many people spend more time in planning the wedding than they do in planning the marriage.

Zig Ziglar

Gay marriage will be universally accepted in time. But if I may be so bold as to say to gays and lesbians, don't wait for that time to arrive. Just as my father and his generation did not 'wait' for their civil rights, nor should you. The toothpaste ain't going back in the tube. The tide has turned.

John Ridley

I think long-lasting, healthy relationships are more important than the idea of marriage. At the root of every successful marriage is a strong partnership.

Carson Daly

A word of encouragement from a teacher to a child can change a life. A word of encouragement from a spouse can save a marriage. A word of encouragement from a leader can inspire a person to reach her potential.

John C. Maxwell

Earlier, my priority was only work. I worked like a dog before I got married. After marriage, once you have a baby, time management is difficult. Your responsibilities change, your priorities change. And you have to concentrate on them if you have to work out your life. Your career is just a part of your life. For me, my family is my life.

Kajol

When people get married because they think it's a long-time love affair, they'll be divorced very soon, because all love affairs end in disappointment. But marriage is a recognition of a spiritual identity.

Joseph Campbell

We cannot insist only on issues related to abortion, gay marriage and the use of contraceptive methods. The teaching of the church is clear, and I am a son of the church, but it is not necessary to talk about these issues all the time.

Pope Francis

I want a happy marriage and whatever it takes to achieve that. But I think the main prerequisite would have to be respect. He would have to respect me and vice-versa. And, that would be more important than being in love. I think respect really goes a long way. And he would have to keep me happy. And he'd have to be very, very, secure.

Shilpa Shetty

Marriage is the most natural state of man, and... the state in which you will find solid happiness.

Benjamin Franklin

I think that gay marriage should be between a man and a woman.

Arnold Schwarzenegger

If your neighbor has a completely different view on

abortion, gay marriage, stem cell research, all of those things, you still are both Americans. Neither one of you is necessarily more patriotic than the other. Neither loves their country any more than the other one does.

Phil McGraw

Marriage is like putting your hand into a bag of snakes in the hope of pulling out an eel.

Leonardo da Vinci

Another argument, vaguer and even less persuasive, is that gay marriage somehow does harm to heterosexual marriage. I have yet to meet anyone who can explain to me what this means. In what way would allowing same-sex partners to marry diminish the marriages of heterosexual couples?

Ted Olson

We will see a breakdown of the family and family values if we decide to approve same-sex marriage, and if we decide to establish homosexuality as an acceptable alternative lifestyle with all the benefits that go with equating it with the heterosexual lifestyle.

Jerry Falwell

Gay rights is just a matter of time. Look at the polls. Worrying about gay marriage, let alone gay civil unions or gay employment rights, is a middle-age issue. Young people just can't see the problem. At worst, gays are going to win this one just by waiting until the opposition dies off.

Gail Collins

Marriage is for women the commonest mode of livelihood, and the total amount of undesired sex endured by women is probably greater in marriage than in prostitution.

Bertrand Russell

Friendship is two-sided. It isn't a friend just because someone's doing something nice for you. That's a nice person. There's friendship when you do for each other. It's like marriage - it's two-sided.

John Wooden

Finding good partners is the key to success in anything: in business, in marriage and, especially, in investing.

Robert Kiyosaki

If a relationship is going wrong, if a marriage is going wrong, the answer cannot simply be to say, 'You can't

afford to break up because you are going to lose the house.'
The answer has to be only one thing, which is 'I love you.'

Rory Stewart

The irrationality of disgust suggests it is unreliable as a
source of moral insight. There may be good arguments
against gay marriage, partial-birth abortions and human
cloning, but the fact that some people find such acts to be
disgusting should carry no weight.

Paul Bloom

Marriage is not a noun; it's a verb. It isn't something you
get. It's something you do. It's the way you love your
partner every day.

Barbara de Angelis

Well I don't know that I'm okay any more than anyone else
is okay, I lead a happy life and a very full one - I have a
happy marriage and my kids are all cheerful, and no one is
finding fault with me, personally.

L. Ron Hubbard

I support gay marriage. I believe they have a right to be as
miserable as the rest of us.

Kinky Friedman

It becomes dangerous for somebody who doesn't want their boss to know their sexual preference to use online networks to push for laws supporting gay marriage or same-sex partner rights if they can't do so with a pseudonym.

Rebecca MacKinnon

Nobody should mistreat anybody... what I think this reveals is that - the interviewer that asked me these questions even used the words with me, 'I think your views are destructive' - so what that shows me is that all of us who really think deeply about social issues, like gay marriage, and abortion, and homosexuality, have convictions on issues.

Kirk Cameron

Ultimately, I believe the only secret to a happy marriage is choosing the right person. Life is a series of choices, right?

Michelle Pfeiffer

Gay marriage is going to happen. It must.

Lady Gaga

The government shouldn't be involved in this because it's very simple. If you don't believe in same-sex marriage, then don't marry somebody of the same sex.

Wanda Sykes

What I believe is that marriage is between a man and a woman, but what I also believe is that we have an obligation to make sure that gays and lesbians have the rights of citizenship that afford them visitations to hospitals, that allow them to be, to transfer property between partners, to make certain that they're not discriminated on the job.

Barack Obama

Marriage equality is about more than just marriage. It's about something greater. It's about acceptance.

Charlize Theron

Love is not weakness. It is strong. Only the sacrament of marriage can contain it.

Boris Pasternak

As I grew up and began identifying myself as a feminist, there were plenty of issues that continued to make me question marriage: the father 'giving' the bride away, women taking their husband's last name, the white dress, the vows promising to 'obey' the groom. And that only covers the wedding.

Jessica Valenti

Ultimately, my greatest achievement is maintaining my career while sustaining a happy marriage and kids.

Melina Kanakaredes

Marriage is a wonderful institution, but who would want to live in an institution?

H. L. Mencken

Love and marriage are wonderful arenas in which to place a character. We are most likely to risk our morals and beliefs while in love. Betrayal gives tremendous insights into a character as well.

Anita Shreve

Psychology is much bigger than just medicine, or fixing unhealthy things. It's about education, work, marriage - it's even about sports. What I want to do is see psychologists working to help people build strengths in all these domains.

Martin Seligman

As to marriage or celibacy, let a man take which course he will, he will be sure to repent.

Socrates

Remember that creating a successful marriage is like farming: you have to start over again every morning.

H. Jackson Brown, Jr.

I adore the theater and I am a painter. I think the two are made for a marriage of love. I will give all my soul to prove this once more.

Marc Chagall

Sometimes I bust out and do things so permanent. Like tattoos and marriage.

Drew Barrymore

Courtship is to marriage, as a very witty prologue to a very dull play.

William Congreve

You're not just going out there, maybe sacrificing your own life. There's also sacrifices still going on at home. You can serve in the military and have a good marriage, but you just need to be aware of it so you can take those steps to take care of it.

Chris Kyle

They say marriage will change you but it didn't change me. Being in love changed me.

R. Kelly

You know, real life doesn't just suddenly resolve itself. You have to keep working at it. Democracy, marriage, friendship. You can't just say, 'She's my best friend.' That's not a given, it's a process.

Viggo Mortensen

It's only fair that stable gay relationships of long standing should have the same rights and responsibilities as married couples. I know the image of gay marriage is to some people horrific and ludicrous.

Ian Mckellen

Mama and Daddy King represent the best in manhood and womanhood, the best in a marriage, the kind of people we are trying to become.

Coretta Scott King

Rituals, anthropologists will tell us, are about transformation. The rituals we use for marriage, baptism or inaugurating a president are as elaborate as they are because we associate the ritual with a major life passage, the crossing of a critical threshold, or in other words, with transformation.

Abraham Verghese

Marriage brings one into fatal connection with custom and tradition, and traditions and customs are like the wind and weather, altogether incalculable.

Soren Kierkegaard

If you cannot work on the marriage or the women is a moron, staying married and cheating makes the most sense because divorce is disruptive to the family life and your bank account.

Al Goldstein

I'm not for gay marriage, but I'm not for discriminating against people.

Joel Osteen

May this marriage be full of laughter, our every day in paradise.

Rumi

But the key to our marriage is the capacity to give each other a break. And to realize that it's not how our similarities work together; it's how our differences work together.

Michael J. Fox

Same-sex marriage is not the final nail in the coffin for traditional marriage. It is just another road sign toward the substitution of government for God. Every moral discussion now pits the wisest moral arbiters among us - the Supreme Court, President Obama - against traditional religion.

Ben Shapiro

American couples have gone to such lengths to avoid the interference of in-laws that they have to pay marriage counselors to interfere between them.

Florence King

Particularly black Americans, many of them, from quotes that I have seen and conversations I've had, are sort of insulted that the civil rights movement is being hijacked - the rhetoric of the civil rights movement is being hijacked for something like same sex marriage. Black Americans tend to have a higher degree of religiosity.

Gary Bauer

In our ecclesiastical region there are priests who don't baptize the children of single mothers because they weren't conceived in the sanctity of marriage. These are today's hypocrites. Those who clericalize the church. Those who separate the people of God from salvation.

Pope Francis

Marriage is like life - it is a field of battle, not a bed of roses.

Robert Louis Stevenson

I'm 0 for 3 with marriage - the scoreboard doesn't lie, never has. So what we all have is a marriage of the heart. To sully or contaminate or radically disrespect this union with a shameful contract is something that I will leave to the amateurs and the Bible grippers.

Charlie Sheen

Before marriage, many couples are very much like people rushing to catch an airplane; once aboard, they turn into passengers. They just sit there.

J. Paul Getty

Little children are still the symbol of the eternal marriage between love and duty.

George Eliot

The Obama administration now has regulations that tells them that they can no longer promote marriage to these young girls. They can no longer promote marriage as a way of avoiding poverty and bad choices that they make in their life. They can no longer even teach abstinence education. They have to be neutral with respect to how people behave.

Rick Santorum

I'm done with men... I'm going to be alone. I have no luck with relationships. I don't think I'm made for marriage.

Halle Berry

In a way, fraud in business is no different from infidelity in marriage or plagiarism in scholarly work. Even people committed to high moral standards succumb.

Miroslav Volf

But the fact that same-sex marriage is still an issue is insane. Thinking love knows a sex is ridiculous.

Garret Dillahunt

A wife lasts only for the length of the marriage, but an ex-wife is there for the rest of your life.

Jim Samuels

The problem with marriage is that it ends every night after making love, and it must be rebuilt every morning before breakfast.

Gabriel Garcia Marquez

Almost no one is foolish enough to imagine that he automatically deserves great success in any field of activity; yet almost everyone believes that he automatically deserves success in marriage.

Sydney J. Harris

Marriage: a ceremony in which rings are put on the finger of the lady and through the nose of the gentleman.

Herbert Spencer

Obama sees himself as such a huge change that he can be cautious about other societal changes. But what he doesn't realize is that legalizing gay marriage is like electing a black president. Before you do it, it seems inconceivable. Once it's done, you can't remember what all the fuss was about.

Maureen Dowd

I was totally surprised by the spread of the legalization of same-sex marriage. In just my lifetime we have gone from a taboo to even talk about homosexuality, to the sanction by governments of homosexual marriage. Few such large social considerations have ever before been turned over in such a short time.

John Naisbitt

Gay marriage won't be more of an issue 25 years from now than interracial marriage is today.

Jared Polis

There is, hidden or flaunted, a sword between the sexes till an entire marriage reconciles them.

C. S. Lewis

Brought up to respect the conventions, love had to end in marriage. I'm afraid it did.

Bette Davis

Marriage, in its truest sense, is a partnership of equals, with neither exercising dominion over the other, but, rather, with each encouraging and assisting the other in whatever responsibilities and aspirations he or she might have.

Gordon B. Hinckley

Marriage is a coming together for better or for worse, hopefully enduring, and intimate to the degree of being sacred.

William O. Douglas

I could be wrong, but I think heterosexual marriage is threatened more by heterosexuals. I don't know why gay marriage challenges my marriage in any way.

Elizabeth Edwards

I love the concept of togetherness and the entwinement of marriage.

William Shatner

No person connected with me by blood or marriage will be appointed to office.

Rutherford B. Hayes

Even though people may be well known, they hold in their hearts the emotions of a simple person for the moments that are the most important of those we know on earth: birth, marriage and death.

Jackie Kennedy

A woman asking 'Am I good? Am I satisfied?' is extremely selfish. The less women fuss about themselves, the less they talk to other women, the more they try to please their husbands, the happier the marriage is going to be.

Barbara Cartland

Marriage has a unique place because it speaks of an absolute faithfulness, a covenant between radically different persons, male and female; and so it echoes the absolute covenant of God with his chosen, a covenant between radically different partners.

Rowan Williams

Usually, the fairy tale ends with the girl marrying the prince. But mine started as soon as the marriage was over.

Diane von Furstenberg

I don't know if I believe in marriage. I believe in family, love and children.

Penelope Cruz

I don't support gay marriage, but I also don't support a

constitutional amendment banning it. However, I do support same sex unions that would give gay couples all the rights, privileges and protections of marriage.

Bob Casey, Jr.

I don't think that a same-sex marriage is the way God intended it to be.

Joel Osteen

I haven't looked at marriage in the conventional sense, as far as settling down. I look at it as putting faith in another person, which has always been hard for me to do.

Marilyn Manson

Marriage is this grand madness, and I think if people knew that, they would perhaps take it more seriously.

Bono

I was against gay marriage until I realized I didn't have to get one.

James Carville

I should have been out there having a wild time like all the other girls my age, but I wasn't. I was going home every night to what was, initially, a very happy marriage.

Amanda Holden

I tried marriage. I'm 0 for 3 with the marriage thing. So, being a ballplayer - I believe in numbers. I'm not going 0 for 4. I'm not wearing a golden sombrero.

Charlie Sheen

More belongs to marriage than four legs in a bed.

Rainer Maria Rilke

You know, my friends, with what a brave carouse I made a Second Marriage in my house; favored old barren reason from my bed, and took the daughter of the vine to spouse.

Omar Khayyam

The mark of a good marriage is partnership and continuing to feel inspired by your spouse. I had that with Tao. But the end is not necessarily the tragedy. Staying in a relationship that is no longer working is the tragedy. Living unhappily - that's the tragedy.

Olivia Wilde

Marriage is a reflection of your life in general: how you treat people, how you argue, how secure you are in your own thoughts. How vehemently do you argue your point of view? With what disdain do you view the other's point of view?

William Shatner

The first breath of adultery is the freest; after it, constraints aping marriage develop.

John Updike

Every marriage tends to consist of an aristocrat and a peasant. Of a teacher and a learner.

John Updike

The value of marriage is not that adults produce children but that children produce adults.

Peter De Vries

Old white guys can be a funny bunch, can't they? The same anti-same-sex marriage, anti-affirmative action cadre can flower into the biggest supporters of 'equality' the minute they get a whiff of minority empowerment.

John Ridley

I think that marriage is, dare I say it, between a man and a woman, hopefully for life and there are all sorts of other relationships which should be acknowledged and recognised, but I don't know that they can be recognised as marriage.

Tony Abbott

I only gave out my opinion that same sex marriage is against the law of God.

Manny Pacquiao

I met my wife in Bombay at an official function. And then we courted for three years. That's a great old term, 'courting.' And we had to do it quietly, of course, because you would know the difficulties one might have with Indian parents. She was advised by her father that people in the West don't take marriage seriously.

Glenn Turner

I came seriously close to getting married four times, and

each time I backed off in fear or for one reason or another. Each occasion was different, but in hindsight when I look at the people involved, it wasn't a bad thing what I did. I think it may have been more complex had the marriage taken place.

Ratan Tata

Children are supposed to help hold a marriage together. They do this in a number of ways. For instance, they demand so much attention that a husband and wife, concentrating on their children, fail to notice each other's faults.

Richard Armour

A liberated woman is one who has sex before marriage and a job after.

Gloria Steinem

The most happy marriage I can picture or imagine to myself would be the union of a deaf man to a blind woman.

Samuel Taylor Coleridge

Marriage is almost as old as dirt, and it was defined in the garden between Adam and Eve. One man, one woman for life till death do you part. So I would never attempt to try to redefine marriage. And I don't think anyone else should either. So do I support the idea of gay marriage? No, I don't.

Kirk Cameron

After 45 years of marriage, when I have an argument with my wife, if we don't agree, we do what she wants. But, when we agree, we do what I want!

Jacques Pepin

I honestly believe you can never tell if a relationship is going to last. In my own marriage, which is going on 14 years, I don't think of it as 'I'm going to be with this person forever.' Instead, I think of more like, 'I'll probably be with this person for the next six weeks. Then I'll re-evaluate.'

Michael Ian Black

Wit is the sudden marriage of ideas which, before their union, were not perceived to have any relation.

Mark Twain

We sleep in separate rooms, we have dinner apart, we take

separate vacations - we're doing everything we can to keep our marriage together.

Rodney Dangerfield

I've yet to be on a campus where most women weren't worrying about some aspect of combining marriage, children, and a career. I've yet to find one where many men were worrying about the same thing.

Gloria Steinem

The sad truth is that the civil rights movement cannot be reborn until we identify the causes of black suffering, some of them self-inflicted. Why can't black leaders organize rallies around responsible sexuality, birth within marriage, parents reading to their children and students staying in school and doing homework?

Henry Louis Gates

To me, marriage is really important and what we build families on. That's why gay marriage is really important.

Margaret Cho

Gay marriage acceptance is happening in the blink of an eye.

P. J. O'Rourke

In my mind, marriage is a spiritual partnership and union in which we willingly give and receive love, create and share intimacy, and open ourselves to be available and accessible to another human being in order to heal, learn and grow.

Iyanla Vanzant

The moral code of Heaven for both men and women is complete chastity before marriage and full fidelity after marriage.

Ezra Taft Benson

Now that virtually every career is an option for ambitious girls, it can no longer be considered regressive or reactionary to reintroduce discussion of marriage and motherhood to primary education. We certainly do not want to return to the simplistic duality of home economics classes for girls and wood shop for boys.

Camille Paglia

There is a lot of healing going on. Really! More people are vegetarians, more are in the green movement, more of us are tearing down the old paradigms and embracing same-sex marriage, single motherhood, men raising babies.

Iyanla Vanzant

On the one hand, the idea of marriage and the sort of traditional family life repulses me. But on the other hand, I long for it, you know what I mean? I'm constantly in conflict with things. And it is because of my past and my upbringing and the journey that I've been on.

Madonna Ciccone

I know one husband and wife who, whatever the official reasons given to the court for the break up of their marriage, were really divorced because the husband believed that nobody ought to read while he was talking and the wife that nobody ought to talk while she was reading.

Vera Brittain

You know, Republicans should have a consistent philosophy. And if your philosophy is about limited government and not intruding in people's lives, you shouldn't just inconveniently take a social issue like gay marriage and say, 'Well, unless we think - actually we should be intruding your life.'

Mark McKinnon

If we really want to cherish religious freedom, people who want to believe that same-sex marriage should take place, they have a right to believe that, and people who want to believe it's inappropriate, we should not demonize those people - if we really believe in religious liberty.

Foster Friess

The one charm about marriage is that it makes a life of deception absolutely necessary for both parties.

Oscar Wilde

My decision to end my marriage was such a risk to lose ratings and lose my fan base. I had to take that risk for my inner peace and to be happy with myself.

Kim Kardashian

I would say that the surest measure of a man's or a woman's maturity is the harmony, style, joy, and dignity he creates in his marriage, and the pleasure and inspiration he provides for his spouse.

Benjamin Spock

Marriage equality is a term so ridiculous on its face that when you hear it mentioned, you would think you were in Riyadh. Years from now, perhaps we can lose the equality part, the same-sex part and call it what it is - marriage.

Henry Rollins

Marriage is like a game of chess except the board is flowing water, the pieces are made of smoke and no move you make will have any effect on the outcome.

Jerry Seinfeld

How marriage ruins a man! It is as demoralizing as cigarettes, and far more expensive.

Oscar Wilde

One should believe in marriage as in the immortality of the soul.

Honore de Balzac

I think like any marriage, especially when you've had divorced parents like myself; you want to try even harder to make it work.

Princess Diana

First love is first love, first marriage is first marriage, disappointment is disappointment.

Maximilian Schell

The great marriages are partnerships. It can't be a great marriage without being a partnership.

Helen Mirren

I read somewhere that Mitt and I have a 'storybook marriage.' Well, in the storybooks I read, there were never long, long, rainy winter afternoons in a house with five boys screaming at once. And those storybooks never seemed to have chapters called MS or breast cancer.

Ann Romney

If you've gone into a marriage and you haven't been clear about how you're going to handle money, how you want to raise kids, who is going to work or stay home or what have you, then you've set yourself up for failure.

Phil McGraw

The secret of a good marriage is forgiving your partner for

marrying you in the first place.

Sacha Guitry

To enter upon the marriage union is one of the most deeply important events of life. It cannot be too prayerfully treated. Our happiness, our usefulness, our living for God or for ourselves afterwards, are often most intimately connected with our choice. Therefore, in the most prayerful manner, this choice should be made.

George Muller

I think growing up in a big family taught me a lot of problem solving and how to share and compromise, and that's been helpful in my marriage.

Sarah Jessica Parker

When I went to college, as much as my parents emphasized academic achievement, they emphasized marriage even more. They told me that the most eligible women marry young to get a 'good man' before they are all taken.

Sheryl Sandberg

God invented concubinage, satan marriage.

Francis Picabia

I have a very happy marriage and friends who keep my feet on the ground. But looking for satisfaction in life is difficult. Maybe being happy is as simple as not being unhappy.

Jasper Carrott

The details surrounding both my marriage and subsequent filing for divorce are private, and I had hoped to keep them that way for the sake of my family.

Eminem

Anyone who thinks that the vice-president can take a position independent of the president of his administration simply has no knowledge of politics or government. You are his choice in a political marriage, and he expects your absolute loyalty.

Hubert H. Humphrey

Even in the common affairs of life, in love, friendship, and marriage, how little security have we when we trust our happiness in the hands of others!

William Hazlitt

May these vows and this marriage be blessed.

Rumi

I put my career in second place throughout both my marriages and it suffered. I don't regret it. You make choices. If you want a good marriage, you must pay attention to that. If you want to be independent, go ahead. You can't have it all.

Lauren Bacall

Marriage is miserable unless you find the right person that is your soulmate and that takes a lot of looking.

Marvin Gaye

In mid-life the man wants to see how irresistible he still is to younger women. How they turn their hearts to stone and more or less commit a murder of their marriage I just don't know, but they do.

Earl Warren

The trend of opinion among eugenists is that we must make marriage more difficult. Certainly no one who is not a desirable parent should be permitted to produce progeny.

Nikola Tesla

A key to keeping your husband is getting him to miss you. That keeps a marriage fresh.

Tori Amos

Alzheimer's disease is never an 'accident' in a marriage. It falls under the purview of God's sovereignty. In the case of someone with Alzheimer's, this means God's unconditional and sacrificial love has an opportunity to be even more gloriously displayed in a life together.

Joni Eareckson Tada

I'm the only man in the world with a marriage licence made out to whom it may concern.

Mickey Rooney

When I talk about the importance of the institution of marriage, I think of the commitment and the significance of standing in front of those closest to you and promising fidelity to your partner 'til death do you part.'

Mark Udall

A good marriage is different to a happy marriage.

Debra Winger

The institution of marriage works better when there's a spiritual connection. If you're marrying just for the sake of the woman, then you may lose interest in each other very soon. When we marry in the interest of the Holy Spirit with the intention of serving God and humanity, then it gives a much larger perspective.

A. R. Rahman

The Hindu marriage may be described as the union of two families. In this union, there is no room for petty ambitions and personal ego-trips. What is involved is love for the entire family that one is marrying into.

Dada Vaswani

We can't destroy the inequities between men and women until we destroy marriage.

Robin Morgan

When I think of a merry, happy, free young girl - and look

at the ailing, aching state a young wife generally is doomed to - which you can't deny is the penalty of marriage.

Queen Victoria

What is marriage but prostitution to one man instead of many?

Angela Carter

The sum and substance of female education in America, as in England, is training women to consider marriage as the sole object in life, and to pretend that they do not think so.

Harriet Martineau

During the periods in my marriage when I chose to stay home with my kids rather than work as an attorney, it caused me no end of anxiety. Despite the fact that I knew I was contributing to our family by caring for our children, I still felt that my worth was less because I wasn't earning.

Ayelet Waldman

I find it extremely ironic that Bush says that personal opinion should not be a tool in the interpretation of the Constitution, when he's the one who's lobbying for a

Constitutional amendment banning gay marriage. If that doesn't stem from personal opinion, I don't know what does.

Jessi Klein

The most important thing for a good marriage is to learn how to argue peaceably.

Anita Ekberg

It was the courts, of course, that took away prayer from our schools, that took away Bible reading from our schools. It's the courts that gave us same-sex marriage. So it is quite a battlefield, and the Supreme Court is the highest court in the land.

Rod Parsley

Many a good hanging prevents a bad marriage.

William Shakespeare

There is no subject on which more dangerous nonsense is talked and thought than marriage.

George Bernard Shaw

In almost every marriage there is a selfish and an unselfish partner. A pattern is set up and soon becomes inflexible, of one person always making the demands and one person always giving way.

Iris Murdoch

Whenever a husband and wife begin to discuss their marriage they are giving evidence at a coroner's inquest.

H. L. Mencken

In every marriage more than a week old, there are grounds for divorce. The trick is to find, and continue to find, grounds for marriage.

Robert Anderson

Marriage is the death of hope.

Woody Allen

Staying married may have long-term benefits. You can elicit much more sympathy from friends over a bad marriage than you ever can from a good divorce.

P. J. O'Rourke

Mr. Christ, I read you as an infinitely patient entity who, as they say, often works in mysterious ways, a rebel unafraid to take the tougher, less traveled paths. Seems to me you're playing the long game. Is that why more states are coming out in favor of marriage equality? Is that why the Affordable Care Act is now with us?

Henry Rollins

I would love to have the same rights as everybody else. I would love, I don't care if it's called marriage. I don't care if it's called, you know, domestic partnership. I don't care what it's called.

Ellen DeGeneres

My view is that marriage is a relationship between a man and a woman. That's the position I've had for some time, and I don't intend to make any adjustments at this point... Or ever, by the way.

Mitt Romney

And let me make this very clear - unlike President Obama, I will not raise taxes on the middle class. As president, I will protect the sanctity of life. I will honor the institution of marriage. And I will guarantee America's first liberty: the freedom of religion.

Mitt Romney

It takes a lot of work to put together a marriage, to put together a family and a home.

Elizabeth Edwards

Our Nation must defend the sanctity of marriage.

George W. Bush

A sense of humor is great - it goes a long, long way in a marriage.

Chris Rock

An affair now and then is good for a marriage. It adds spice, stops it from getting boring... I ought to know.

Bette Davis

You can't have a happy family if you don't have a happy marriage.

Jeremy Sisto

Feminism is dated? Yes, for privileged women like my daughter and all of us here today, but not for most of our sisters in the rest of the world who are still forced into premature marriage, prostitution, forced labor - they have children that they don't want or they cannot feed.

Isabel Allende

There is nothing wrong with your marriage if you're dealing with bills and kids and the broken garbage disposal and in-laws and work demands. That's a normal marriage.

Phil McGraw

One of the things I discover a lot in marriage counseling is the husband or wife trying to get their spiritual thirst quenched by their partner; I think that's a real common mistake that we make.

Max Lucado

If dysfunction means that a family doesn't work, then every family ambles into some arena in which that happens, where relationships get strained or even break down entirely. We fail each other or disappoint each other. That goes for parents, siblings, kids, marriage partners - the whole enchilada.

Mary Karr

After a while in marriage, it doesn't work anymore. There is something missing, there is something wrong. There are few marriages that stay alive forever. We like something, and after a while, we hate what we used to love.

Monica Bellucci

Never stay in a bad marriage, and don't hang around with psycho coke fiends.

Joe Rogan

There is no loneliness like that of a failed marriage.

Alexander Theroux

During last night's debate, John Kerry and John Edwards were so friendly to each other some political experts think that they may end up running together. In fact Kerry and Edwards were so friendly, President Bush accused them of planning a gay marriage.

Conan O'Brien

When you're a father in a marriage, you sort of become the mother's assistant. And you sort of get a list from her every

day and you run down the list and it feels very much like a
chore.

Louis C. K.

Homosexuality is against nature. Sexual expression is
permitted only within marriage, between man and woman,
male and female. Anything else is an abnormality and is
against nature.

Pope Shenouda III

I grew up in a Hindu household but went to a Roman
Catholic school. I grew up with a mother who said, 'I'll
arrange a marriage for you at 18,' but she also said that we
could achieve anything we put our minds to an encourage
us to dream of becoming prime minister or president.

Indra Nooyi

A significant fraction of evangelical voters appear more
likely to ignore the candidates' specific economic and
foreign policy platforms in favor of concerns about gay
marriage or abortion.

Lawrence M. Krauss

In interviews I gave early on in my career, I was quoted as

saying it was possible to have it all: a dynamic job, marriage, and children. In some respects, I was a social adolescent.

Jessica Savitch

It takes two to make a marriage a success and only one to make it a failure.

Herbert Samuel

It only took one text message to change my life. That's when I discovered my loving husband had been unfaithful. His infidelities ended our marriage.

Garcelle Beauvais

Even prior to marriage and motherhood, it's always been about prioritising and focusing on what you can commit to. That's been my approach to every aspect of my life, be it my relationships or my professional commitments.

Aishwarya Rai Bachchan

Since the dawn of time, traditional marriage - the union between one man and one woman - has been the building block of civilization, and at no point in our nation's history has that foundation been under more severe attack than now.

Jim DeMint

There are going to be peaks and valleys in everything - in your marriage, in your job, in your life. So just enjoy the peaks and ride out the valleys. Just try not to do anything too rash.

Ricky Schroder

I think marriage is a beautiful thing. I'm still a supporter of it.

Nas

We'll sort of get over the marriage first and then maybe look at the kids. But obviously we want a family so we'll have to start thinking about that.

Prince William

After lengthy consideration, my views have evolved sufficiently to support marriage equality legislation. This position doesn't require any religious denomination to alter any of its tenets; it simply forbids government from discrimination regarding who can marry whom.

Tim Johnson

Redefining marriage will have huge implications for what is taught in our schools, and for wider society. It will redefine society since the institution of marriage is one of the fundamental building blocks of society. The repercussions of enacting same-sex marriage into law will be immense.

Keith O'Brien

Well, marriage doesn't function in the way it used to in terms of deciding our fate, but it's in our heads, and it determines a lot of our actions. Like, right now, if you think about gay marriage - and they just started having the first gay marriages in New York - it shows what a potent idea marriage remains for people.

Jeffrey Eugenides

People ask what the secret of a happy marriage is. If there is one, it's 'don't talk about it.'

Jane Asher

I'd love to have First Lady Michelle Obama over and ask, 'How do you make your marriage work?' I think the president is sexy as all get-out, but he has got to get on her nerves some kind of way. He's this wonderful, powerful man, but she sees him leaving his socks on the floor.

Sherri Shepherd

Obama is for same-sex marriage. If the president is saying that, then who am I to go the other way?

Curtis Jackson

Marriage helps young couples to raise themselves towards God. The bond of marriage unites two souls so firmly that though they are physically two separate entities, their souls are merged into one harmonious whole.

Dada Vaswani

With marriage and fatherhood, I've finally found two fixed points in my life. They've taught me patience. They've also taught me that I don't need to feel guilty about being happy. My emotional seasons are less extreme.

Pete Wentz

Marriage is another trap. If you are someone who likes independence, it's another stamp against that. And you have to swear to fidelity.

Carla Bruni

When you see a merger between two giants in a declining industry, it can look like the financial version of a couple having a baby to save a marriage.

Adam Davidson

I don't support gay marriage. I'm just not there, as far as believing in my heart that we should change 2,000 years of social policy in favor of a redefinition of the family.

Matt Salmon

Most modern Indians don't stick to their caste jobs any more. There is more inter-caste marriage, more fluidity, more freedom than ever before. But the outcastes are usually still outcastes, because they are still the ones who tan India's animals, burn its dead, and remove its excrement.

Rose George

Next month, I will celebrate my 30th anniversary of marriage with my beautiful bride, Vicki. Our marriage has been a blessing. I have gained even more respect for the institution over the past 3 decades and will defend it against attack.

Todd Tiahrt

I wasn't looking for another marriage. I had been married before. He is a nice man - a geologist, an Ernest Hemingway type. But Paul and I married because of convention.

Linda McCartney

You can't wake up one day and say 'I'm for gay marriage,' and wake up the next day and say 'I'm against it.' Wake up one day and say, 'I'm pro-choice,' and the next day wake up and say, 'I'm pro-life.' There's no credibility there.

Roger Stone

When I got married in my twenties, I had a happy marriage and happy kids but at some point in time I let it go off the rails; I let it go off the rails.

Stuart Rose

The marriage of a man and woman is the most enduring human institution, honored in all cultures and by every religious faith. It's in this institution that children are meant to be nurtured. We know this after thousands of years of human experience.

Jeff Miller

Does God feel like that same-sex marriage could happen? I don't think anybody who has a connection to God and God's understanding and depth of compassion who's gonna say 'no.'

Greg Boyle

Marriage destroyed my relationship with two wonderful men.

Marilyn Monroe

Marriage is popular because it combines the maximum of temptation with the maximum of opportunity.

George Bernard Shaw

Marriage is good enough for the lower classes: they have facilities for desertion that are denied to us.

George Bernard Shaw

I think what makes our marriage work amid all the glare is that my husband is my best friend. He inspires everything in my life and enables me to do the best that I can. I want to hang out with him more than anyone.

Faith Hill

Friendship is the marriage of the soul, and this marriage is liable to divorce.

Voltaire

In marriage, a man becomes slack and selfish, and undergoes a fatty degeneration of his moral being.

Robert Louis Stevenson

Marriage: A friendship recognized by the police.

Robert Louis Stevenson

Divorce is probably of nearly the same date as marriage. I believe, however, that marriage is some weeks the more ancient.

Voltaire

The Bible is clear - God's definition of marriage is between a man and a woman.

Billy Graham

You can forgive people who do not follow you through a philosophical disquisition; but to find your wife laughing when you had tears in your eyes, or staring when you were in a fit of laughter, would go some way towards a dissolution of the marriage.

Robert Louis Stevenson

I don't think marriage is a civil right, but I think that being able to transfer property is a civil right.

Barack Obama

I opposed the Defense of Marriage Act in 1996. It should be repealed and I will vote for its repeal on the Senate floor. I will also oppose any proposal to amend the U.S. Constitution to ban gays and lesbians from marrying.

Barack Obama

I think there are a whole host of things that are civil rights, and then there are other things - such as traditional marriage - that, I think, express a community's concern and regard for a particular institution.

Barack Obama

My marriage is on the rocks again, yeah, my wife just broke up with her boyfriend.

Rodney Dangerfield

As a former resident with strong personal and ministry ties to the North Star State, I pray that the good people of Minnesota will show their support for God's definition of marriage, between a man and a woman.

Billy Graham

For it is mutual trust, even more than mutual interest that holds human associations together. Our friends seldom profit us but they make us feel safe. Marriage is a scheme to accomplish exactly that same end.

H. L. Mencken

I respect the fact that many denominations have different points of view with respect to gay marriage and they can hold that in the sanctity in the place of their religion and not bless them or solemnize them.

Colin Powell

In terms of the legal matter of creating a contract between two people that's called marriage, and allowing them to live together with the protection of law, it seems to me is the way we should be moving in this country.

Colin Powell

Marriage is a very good thing, but I think it's a mistake to make a habit out of it.

W. Somerset Maugham

I often say that if you want to really want to understand the contract of marriage, just ask anyone who has been divorced. The marriage contract is one of property rights. Or maybe you can look in the Bible to see what Adam had to say about divorce, since Eve was his second wife.

Harvey Fierstein

A bride at her second marriage does not wear a veil. She wants to see what she is getting.

Helen Rowland

State-sanctioned marriage is a civil contract, period. A contract is not a judgment of moral value. It is a legal agreement between two parties that testifies to a meeting of minds between those consenting entities. It is not a religious act or rite and so has nothing to do with Adam and Eve or Steve or even Harvey.

Harvey Fierstein

Early on in my life, I had a broken soul. I was abused by my father, abandoned by my mother and ended up in a destructive first marriage. By the time I was 23, I was broken in my soul. I didn't know how to think right. I felt wrong about everything. But God stepped into my life, and I came out on the other side and didn't even smell like smoke.

Joyce Meyer

In marriage do thou be wise: prefer the person before money, virtue before beauty, the mind before the body; then thou hast a wife, a friend, a companion, a second self.

William Penn

I'm most proud of the longevity of my marriage, my kids, and my grandchildren. If you don't have that, you really don't have very much.

Bob Newhart

I think marriage is a boring and fault-ridden contractual obligation.

Henry Rollins

I feel very deeply about the need to respect and tolerate people of different social - or sexual orientation. But at the same time, I believe marriage should be preserved as an institution for one man and one woman.

Mitt Romney

Marriage is give and take. You'd better give it to her or she'll take it anyway.

Joey Adams

Always remember that the most important thing in a good marriage is not happiness, but stability.

Gabriel Garcia Marquez

Marriage must be a relation either of sympathy or of conquest.

George Eliot

Having federal officials, whether judges, bureaucrats, or congressmen, impose a new definition of marriage on the people is an act of social engineering profoundly hostile to liberty.

Ron Paul

Children live in the only successful Marxist state ever created: the family. 'From each according to his ability, to each according to his need' is the family's practice as well as its theory. Even with today's scattershot patterns of marriage and parenting, a family is collectivist to a more than North Korean degree.

P. J. O'Rourke

There is the love and marriage and family kind of happiness, which is exceedingly boring to describe but nonetheless is important to have and dreadful not to have.

P. J. O'Rourke

To an honest judge, the alleged marriage between religion and science is a shallow, empty, spin-doctored sham.

Richard Dawkins

Jazz music is as American as it gets, and so is the U.S.

Postal Service. A Miles Davis stamp is a perfect marriage of two great American institutions.

Henry Rollins

Of course same sex marriage is constitutional! The right to be yourself, to pursue life, liberty, and property, is protected several ways over several amendments. John Boehner should know this.

Henry Rollins

A marriage without conflicts is almost as inconceivable as a nation without crises.

Andre Maurois

Marriage, a market which has nothing free but the entrance.

Michel de Montaigne

Let us be honest with each other. The threat to marriage is not the gays. It is a lack of loving commitment - whether it is found in the form of neglect, indifference, cruelty or adultery, to name just a few manifestations of the loveless desert in which too many marriages come to grief.

Malcolm Turnbull

I'm so wrapped up in my work that it's often impossible to consider other things in my life. My marriage ended in divorce because of this, my relationship with Holly has suffered by this.

Jim Carrey

The secret to a long marriage is to stay gone.

Dolly Parton

In the hands of the ego, marriage is a prison. It is exclusive. It is a place where people are constantly reminded of their failures and limited by the energies of another person. It is rife with judgment and blame.

Marianne Williamson

Marriage is the torment of one, the felicity of two, the strife and enmity of three.

Washington Irving

It is always incomprehensible to a man that a woman should ever refuse an offer of marriage.

Jane Austen

Marriage changes everything.

Marilyn Manson

I like marriage. The idea.

Toni Morrison

Marriage is distinctly and repeatedly excluded from heaven. Is this because it is thought likely to mar the general felicity?

Samuel Butler

Like me, the great majority of Americans wish both to preserve the traditional definition of marriage and to oppose bias and intolerance directed towards gays and lesbians.

Mitt Romney

I think men who have a pierced ear are better prepared for marriage. They've experienced pain and bought jewelry.

Rita Rudner

Woman, or more precisely put, perhaps, marriage, is the representative of life with which you are meant to come to terms.

Franz Kafka

My partner Donald Trump says that married couples should always have a prenuptial agreement. True, a prenuptial is important if one partner is much richer than the other before marriage, but Kim and I don't have one.

Robert Kiyosaki

Political promises are much like marriage vows. They are made at the beginning of the relationship between candidate and voter, but are quickly forgotten.

Dick Gregory

I believe a marriage is between a man and a woman.

George W. Bush

How hard it is to have the beautiful interdependence of marriage and yet be strong in oneself alone.

Anne Morrow Lindbergh

I do not think that marriage is one of my talents. I've been much happier unmarried than married.

Doris Lessing

Marriage is like wine. It is not be properly judged until the second glass.

Douglas William Jerrold

It was a perfect marriage. She didn't want to and he couldn't.

Spike Milligan

Art is a marriage of the conscious and the unconscious.

Jean Cocteau

Before marriage, a man declares that he would lay down his life to serve you; after marriage, he won't even lay down his newspaper to talk to you.

Helen Rowland

Marriage brings up all the things I pushed to the back burner - the fears, the mistrust, the doubts, the insecurities. It's like opening Pandora's box.

Jennifer Aniston

A good marriage is one which allows for change and growth in the individuals and in the way they express their love.

Pearl S. Buck

Marriage is not just spiritual communion, it is also remembering to take out the trash.

Joyce Brothers

Marriage is a very sacred institution and should not be degraded by allowing every other type of relationship to be made equivalent to it.

Benjamin Carson

Marriage is really tough because you have to deal with feelings... and lawyers.

Richard Pryor

I'm also interested in the modern suggestion that you can have a combination of love and sex in a marriage - which no previous society has ever believed.

Alain de Botton

I have never been given to envy - save for the envy I feel toward those people who have the ability to make a marriage work and endure happily.

J. Paul Getty

Love, the quest; marriage, the conquest; divorce, the inquest.

Helen Rowland

Marriage is the miracle that transforms a kiss from a pleasure into a duty.

Helen Rowland

Sticking with a marriage. That's true grit, man.

Jeff Bridges

Our marriage is grounded in the word of God. That's really

it. God is the core of our marriage, and the foundation and the blueprint for it is how we live, and being open and honest and communicating, but ultimately doing what pleases God, and not in a selfish manner.

Candace Cameron Bure

When people say 'marriage' to me... It's always a means to an end. Everyone's so in a rush to define the relationship.

Lady Gaga

Woman was given to man as an helpmeet. That complementary association is ideally portrayed in the eternal marriage of our first parents - Adam and Eve. They labored together; they had children together; they prayed together; and they taught their children the gospel together. This is the pattern God would have all righteous men and women imitate.

Ezra Taft Benson

Perhaps my problem in marriage-and it is the problem of many women-was to want both intimacy and independence. It is a difficult line to walk, yet both needs are important to a marriage.

Hedy Lamarr

Marriage is a big deal, but who's to say I'm not going to pull a Vegas and get married to see what it's like for a minute?

Lindsay Lohan

Divorce these days is a religious vow, as if the proper offspring of marriage.

Tertullian

If variety is the spice of life, marriage is the big can of leftover Spam.

Johnny Carson

Those who condemn gay marriage, yet are silent or indifferent to the breakdown of marriage and divorce, are, in my view, missing the real issue.

Malcolm Turnbull

Marriage is the tomb of love.

Giacomo Casanova

The clearest explanation for the failure of any marriage is

that the two people are incompatible; that is, that one is male and the other female.

Anna Quindlen

If we abandon marriage, we abandon the family.

Michael Enzi

Determine that there will never be anything that will come between you that will disrupt your marriage. Make it work. Resolve to make it work.

Gordon B. Hinckley

After marriage, the other man's wife looks more beautiful.

Navjot Singh Sidhu

Pink Floyd is like a marriage that's on a permanent trial separation.

Rick Wright

If there were no immortality there would be no need for temples. There would be no need for eternal marriage if there were no eternity.

Gordon B. Hinckley

The priesthood is a marriage. People often start by falling in love, and they go on for years without realizing that love must change into some other love which is so unlike it that it can hardly be recognized as love at all.

Iris Murdoch

I believe in the institution of marriage, and I intend to keep trying till I get it right.

Richard Pryor

Never ever discount the idea of marriage. Sure, someone might tell you that marriage is just a piece of paper. Well, so is money, and what's more life-affirming than cold, hard cash?

Dennis Miller

The biggest financial pitfall in life is divorce. And the biggest reason for divorce is marriage.

Gene Simmons

It took me a long time to be convinced that marriage was

right for me because I've come from a long line of broken marriages. My parents divorced, and I had two broken marriages myself.

Sylvester Stallone

Nobody ever asks a father how he manages to combine marriage and a career.

Sam Ewing

When our children obey the Lord and go to the temple to receive their blessings and enter into the marriage covenant, they enter into the same order of the priesthood that God instituted in the very beginning with father Adam.

Ezra Taft Benson

When I'm weak, you can be strong; when I'm strong, you can be weak. That's what I believe marriage is.

Gisele Bundchen

The possibility of divorce renders both marriage partners stricter in their observance of the duties they owe to each other. Divorces help to improve morals and to increase the population.

Denis Diderot

Beguiling voices in the world cry out for 'alternative lifestyles' for women. They maintain that some women are better suited for careers than for marriage and motherhood.

Ezra Taft Benson

I don't understand what the big deal is with gay marriage. Get over it, people.

Kristin Chenoweth

If someone wants to marry you outside the temple, whom will you strive to please - God or a mortal? If you insist on a temple marriage, you will be pleasing the Lord and blessing the other party.

Ezra Taft Benson

I firmly believe in marriage. It's a real important decision that takes a lot of dedication and time. If you're thinking about divorce. You shouldn't get married.

Seth Green

Marriage is obsolete and a trap.

Catherine Deneuve

The more time you invest in a marriage, the more valuable it becomes.

Amy Grant

I did commit to myself that I would not jump back into being the workaholic that I can be before I gave myself an honest opportunity to create the marriage of my dreams and to create the beginning of the family of my dreams, and that took a hot second.

Alanis Morissette

Marriage is a good deal like a circus: there is not as much in it as is represented in the advertising.

E. W. Howe

Whether it be a matter of personal relations within a marriage or political initiatives within a peace process, there is no sure-fire do-it-yourself kit.

Seamus Heaney

I'm not convinced about marriage. Divorce is so easy, and

that fact that gay people are not allowed to marry takes much of the meaning out of it. Committing yourself to one person is sacred.

Natalie Portman

In 1989 when I switched from Democrat to Republican, with God as my witness, not one thing changed about what I believed about one man and one woman in a marriage or about diversity of color. That's a good thing.

J. C. Watts

We make no greater voluntary choice in this life than the selection of a marriage partner. This decision can bring eternal happiness and joy. To find sublime fulfillment in marriage, both partners need to be fully committed to the marriage.

James E. Faust

It's volatile, the marriage. Which one isn't? Nothing better than a good, full-on row. Get it all out. Say rude and nasty things. And then be sorry. Genuinely sorry, afterwards.

John Lydon

The sweet companionship of eternal marriage is one of the

greatest blessings God has granted to His children.

Joseph B. Wirthlin

Fear paralyses you - fear of flying, fear of the future, fear of leaving a rubbish marriage, fear of public speaking, or whatever it is.

Annie Lennox

Why is marriage the pinnacle for everyone? People get married for the wrong reasons. We need to start looking at different packages, whether it's living together, or being with six partners, or dedicating your life to taking care of flowers.

Sandra Bullock

Marriage is too interesting an experiment to be tried only once.

Eva Gabor

Marriage? It's like asparagus eaten with vinaigrette or hollandaise, a matter of taste but of no importance.

Francoise Sagan

In my long life I have found peace, joy, and happiness beyond my fondest hopes and dreams. One of the supreme benedictions of my life has been my marriage to an elect daughter of God. I love her with all my heart and soul.

James E. Faust

I'm the person that I always was, but in terms of how I approach my living, I'm not the same person at all. At all. I've buried a child, I've ended a marriage, and the grandson that I was raising is now grown. My family has totally shifted.

Iyanla Vanzant

I have a terrific marriage, but unlike a lot of relationships where they ebb and flow, no matter what happens you fall deeper and deeper in love every day. It's kind of the best thing that can happen to you. It's thrilling.

Hugh Jackman

Right now, I'm not really thinking about marriage.

Adam Lambert

Marriage is a risk; I think it's a great and glorious risk, as long as you embark on the adventure in the same spirit.

Cate Blanchett

Sometimes divorce is better than marriage.

Sumner Redstone

I thought the divorce statistics would never apply to me. I was beyond heartbroken when they did. But I got up and got on with it. I also kept my belief in marriage.

Jennifer Garner

Marriage is a commitment for life. It is a permanent, lifelong relationship.

Dada Vaswani

College is a place to keep warm between high school and an early marriage.

George Gobel

In the 1960s we were fighting to be recognized as equals in the marketplace, in marriage, in education and on the playing field. It was a very exciting, rebellious time.

Marlo Thomas

In marriage, compromise nurtures the relationship.

Tim Allen

Marriage is about the most expensive way for the average man to get laundry done.

Burt Reynolds

Well, my wife and I were married in a toilet - it was a marriage of convenience!

Tommy Cooper

I come from divorce. I'm only doing marriage once. It's not a game for me.

Shia LaBeouf

Love is more pleasant than marriage for the same reason that novels are more amusing than history.

Nicolas Chamfort

I did commit adultery, if adultery is having a relationship

in a marriage with another woman. I learned from that.

Steve Garvey

I think one reason for a successful marriage is laughter. I think laughter gets you through the rough moments in a marriage.

Bob Newhart

It's nice to know you have support. Last night I got a marriage proposal. I just laughed.

Carrie Underwood

The press is just not your friend when it comes to a marriage. That's why we didn't sell the pictures of our wedding, and we got offered millions of dollars for them, millions.

Katy Perry

Who of us is mature enough for offspring before the offspring themselves arrive? The value of marriage is not that adults produce children but that children produce adults.

Peter De Vries

Marriage is a lot of things - a source of love, security, the joy of children, but it's also an interpersonal battlefield, and it's not hard to see why: Take two disparate people, toss them together in often-confined quarters, add the stresses of money and kids - now lather, rinse, repeat for the rest of your natural life. What could go wrong?

Jeffrey Kluger

Unfenced by law, the unmarried lover can quit a bad relationship at any time. But you - the legally married person who wants to escape doomed love - may soon discover that a significant portion of your marriage contract belongs to the State, and that it sometimes takes a very long while for the State to grant you your leave.

Elizabeth Gilbert

If traditional marriage is not the law of the land, the institution of the family will cease to exist.

James Dobson

When we are baptized and confirmed, when brethren are ordained to the priesthood, when we go to the temple and receive our endowment, when we enter into the new and everlasting covenant of eternal marriage - in all these sacred ordinances, we make solemn commitments to keep God's commandments.

Joseph B. Wirthlin

Of all actions of a man's life, his marriage does least concern other people, yet of all actions of our life tis most meddled with by other people.

John Selden

Nothing in life is as good as the marriage of true minds between man and woman. As good? It is life itself.

Pearl S. Buck

The cultural expectation should be if there's infidelity, the marriage is more important than fidelity.

Dan Savage

I don't think there's anything they can say about me that I haven't said about myself already. And I would be an absolute total liar, and my fans would not respect me, if I said that my life and my marriage are perfect. But we absolutely love each other; we have fun together - it's great.

Mary J. Blige

I couldn't think of anything worse than being in an unhappy marriage. It worries me because I've seen it destroy people.

Simon Cowell

I have no difficulty with the recognition of civil unions for non-traditional relationships but I believe in law we should protect the traditional definition of marriage.

Stephen Harper

Adultery - which is the only grounds for divorce in New York - is not grounds for divorce in California. As a matter of fact, adultery in Southern California is grounds for marriage.

Allan Sherman

What I've learned about marriage: You need to have each other's back; you have to be a kind of team going through life.

Tom Petty

I never had a policy about marriage. I got married very young in life and I always think in all relationships, I've always thought that it's counterproductive to have a theory on that.

Jack Nicholson

I always say now that I'm in my blonde years. Because since the end of my marriage, all of my girlfriends have been blonde.

Hugh Hefner

Straight couples don't have to be monogamous to be married or married to be monogamous. Monogamy no more defines marriage than the presence of children does. Monogamy isn't compulsory and its absence doesn't invalidate a marriage.

Dan Savage

I can look back at different times in my life when I felt I could not find my way out of whatever it was. I'm not necessarily talking about marriage, but I wanted to pack it in. I wanted to disappear. A lot of that has to do with being in the public eye.

Amy Grant

I've never understood why we would want to deny all the joys - and the challenges - of marriage to anyone. Which is why I think any loving, committed couple - gay or straight - should be able to get married.

Al Franken

There are many deaf people who couldn't imagine living in a marriage without someone who doesn't speak their language. For me, I believe that hearing or deaf is fine as long as both parties are willing to communicate in each other's language. But if there's no communication, then the marriage, I believe, will be difficult if not doomed.

Marlee Matlin

If I write a book where all I've ever experienced is success, people won't take a positive lesson from it. In being candid, I have to own up to my own failures, both in my marriage and in my work environment.

Sonia Sotomayor

In a bad marriage, friends are the invisible glue. If we have enough friends, we may go on for years, intending to leave, talking about leaving - instead of actually getting up and leaving.

Erica Jong

The submission of her body without love or desire is degrading to the woman's finer sensibility, all the marriage certificates on earth to the contrary notwithstanding.

Margaret Sanger

I love the institution of marriage, and I love my marriage.

Kyle Chandler

Marriage requires a special talent, like acting. Monogamy requires genius.

Warren Beatty

My grandmother was energetic and fearless - a talented poet and songwriter. She was also interested in chemistry and history and medicine, taking care of the people in her hacienda in Mexico, delivering babies. She could have become anything, but this was the 1930s, and she was forced into an arranged marriage.

Salma Hayek

I won't have a traditional marriage; I don't find the value in that anymore. But I am such a hopeless romantic and I really want love and I want a committed relationship, so I am going to reinvent marriage for myself.

Halle Berry

The facts are plain: Religious leaders who preside over marriage ceremonies must and will be guided by what they believe. If they do not wish to celebrate marriages for same-sex couples, that is their right. The Supreme Court says so. And the Charter says so.

Paul Martin

Sobering up was responsible for breaking up my marriage. That's what it couldn't stand.

James Taylor

I believe in traditional marriage and I believe in the Defense of Marriage Act.

Herman Cain

She got the magazine on a Wednesday morning, and on Thursday announced our marriage was over.

David Gest

Any sex outside of the marriage bond between a man and a woman is violating God's law.

Jerry Falwell

I think of marriage as a garden. You have to tend to it. Respect it, take care of it, feed it. Make sure everyone is getting the right amount of, um, sunlight.

Mark Ruffalo

I think the gay community should get smart and drop the word 'marriage.' Do you really need to change every right-wing Christian to make sure you get your equal rights? Eyes on the prize, we should be sticking to getting equal rights.

Ani DiFranco

Marriage can be viewed as the waiting room for death.

Mike Myers

The problem for those who assert biblical authority in support of traditional definitions of marriage is that one could, with equal validity, assert that the lending of money or certain kinds of haircuts are forbidden by God, or that slavery and the subjugation of women are authorized by the Lord.

Jon Meacham

I was born to be married. I just feel comfortable there. I love the idea of being partnered for ever. I love my girlfriend, we've been best friends since I was 18. There's not a thing we haven't been through except for marriage... We've had talks about what we would name our kids since we were in our 20s.

Beth Ditto

Marriage is an institution, and you must be fully committed to it.

Gene Simmons

Just as the unique characteristics of both males and females contribute to the completeness of a marriage relationship, so those same characteristics are vital to the rearing, nurturing, and teaching of children.

David A. Bednar

I yearned for a long, happy marriage with one person.

Ginger Rogers

Brands mature over time, like a marriage. The bond you feel with your spouse is different than when you first met each other. Excitement and discovery are replaced by comfort and depth.

Gary Vaynerchuk

I learned to cook in self-defense. My wife doesn't know what a kitchen is. In the first month of our marriage, she broiled lamb chops 26 nights in a row. Then I took over. I used to mind her not caring about food, but no more - as long as I can eat what I want.

Alan King

My mother had a son from previous marriage and her husband died in Second World War.

Mikhail Baryshnikov

The truth is that many powerful guys have fooled around while working for the people. Dwight Eisenhower, John F. Kennedy, and Warren Harding to name just a few. Grover Cleveland even fathered a child outside of marriage. We all know these things happen. But we don't want them to happen - at least most of us don't. I can't speak for San Francisco.

Bill O'Reilly

A marriage is no amusement but a solemn act, and generally a sad one.

Queen Victoria

Marriage is not simply a romantic union between two people; it's also a political and economic contract of the highest order.

Elizabeth Gilbert

Having had five husbands, I guess I should know a thing or two about marriage.

Joan Collins

I think it's best if there's an amendment that goes on the ballot where the people can weigh in. Every time this issue has gone on the ballot, the people have voted to retain the traditional definition of marriage as recently as California in 2008.

Michele Bachmann

I like marriage. I feel very secure. It helps when you are in love with the person you are married to.

Claire Danes

It is better to be unhappy in love than unhappy in marriage, but some people manage to be both.

Guy de Maupassant

My mother and stepfather were married 43 years, so I have watched a long marriage. I feel like I had a very good role model for that. And, you know, it's just a number.

Jamie Lee Curtis

I think I'm a combination of very simple pleasures and the fact I've read a lot of books. I don't think it's a binary opposition across the board in humans and I think I'm an example that it's not. I'm hosting gay marriage rallies and I have tons of guns at home. There's a lot of middle ground in the world and I'm one of those people.

Dax Shepard

The death of anti-gay hate speech is no doubt being hastened by the head-spinning speed with which gays as a group - to say nothing of gay marriage - are becoming an unremarkable and even quite traditional parts of American life.

Jeffrey Kluger

The media seems to think only abortion and gay marriage are religious issues. Poverty is a moral issue, it's a faith issue, it's a religious issue.

Jim Wallis

Marriage is an institution fits in perfect harmony with the laws of nature; whereas systems of slavery and segregation were designed to brutally oppress people and thereby violated the laws of nature.

Jack Kingston

When I heard the royal family wanted to have me perform in celebration of Prince William's marriage, I knew I had to give them a little something. 'Wet' is the perfect anthem for Prince William or any playa to get the club smokin'.

Snoop Dogg

I'm an advocate for gay marriage. I have more gay friends than Carter has pills.

Patti Stanger

Do I support the idea of gay marriage? No, I don't.

Kirk Cameron

I'm certain that most couples expect to find intimacy in marriage, but it somehow eludes them.

James Dobson

The only day I remember of my parents' marriage was the day my dad walked out. As I stood there at five years old, with my older sister and younger brother, I knew that he was gone.

Ellie Goulding

I'll say this: The media wasn't invited to my marriage, and they're definitely not invited into the divorce.

Ryan Reynolds

The argument that gay marriage doesn't affect straight marriages is a ridiculous red herring: Gay marriage affects society and law in dramatic ways. Religious groups will come under direct assault as federal and state governments move to strip them of their non-profit statuses if they refuse to perform gay marriages.

Ben Shapiro

Most people like to read about intrigue and spies. I hope to provide a metaphor for the average reader's daily life. Most of us live in a slightly conspiratorial relationship with our employer and perhaps with our marriage.

John le Carre

Obama's endorsement of gay marriage is hardly as consequential as Johnson's legislative success on civil rights.

Robert Dallek

When I say things like 'Marriage should be between one man and one woman,' I'm called a bigot.

Rick Santorum

I love Matthew Broderick. Call me crazy, but I love him. We can only be in the marriage we are. We're very devoted to our family and our lives. I love our life. I love that he's the father of my children, and it's because of him that there's this whole other world that I love.

Sarah Jessica Parker

There aren't many great adverts for marriage or parenthood. It always looks so stressful, and that's what I've been scared of. What you don't realise is how much you're going to get back.

Robbie Williams

I was gone so much in my first marriage. I love the moments when I engage with my youngest daughter now. It's not my thing to sit on the ground and play tea party, but I'll do it because it's a moment that will stick with me forever.

Tim Allen

Spiritually, we have marginalized the Bible. We've trivialized marriage, and we've neutralized the church. America today is in great turmoil. It feels like the soul of our nation has been taken from us.

David Jeremiah

I've had marriage proposals, invitations to military balls and even a few prom offers from 18-year-old boys.

Hope Solo

But I will agree that I think that things happen with people in relationships, that you might have been able to enjoy Morocco, say, if you weren't getting out of a bad marriage. You know what I mean?

Robert Downey, Jr.

Coming to terms with the fact that my marriage was a failure was devastating and very difficult. I blamed myself for a lot of things. It took me a very long time to get over it.

Sarah McLachlan

I am fiscally prudent and socially progressive. I believe in protecting a woman's right to choose. I believe in marriage equality.

Andrew Cuomo

There are four stages in a marriage. First there's the affair, then the marriage, then children and finally the fourth stage, without which you cannot know a woman, the divorce.

Norman Mailer

As somebody who, in my second marriage, insisted on a prenuptial agreement, I can also testify that sometimes it is an act of love to chart the exit strategy before you enter the union, in order to make sure that not only you, but your partner as well, knows that there will be no World War III should hearts and minds, for any sad reason, change.

Elizabeth Gilbert

What is fascinating about marriage is why anyone wants to get married.

Alain de Botton

As wonderful as they were, my parents didn't teach me anything about self-discipline, concentration, patience, or focus. If I hadn't had a family myself, I probably never would've done anything. Marriage taught me responsibility.

Dick Van Dyke

The truth is that I'm more afraid of marriage than of death.

Shakira

My mother and father had a terrible marriage. They celebrated their wedding anniversary one year with their friends. Why did they celebrate? Maybe because they had lasted so many years without killing each other.

Marina Abramovic

The corporate right fires up the religious right against gay marriage and abortion and uses their votes to push their deregulation and tax cuts for the rich. It's an old trick. The House of Saud has the same arrangement with the Mullahs in Saudi Arabia.

Adam McKay

My first wife was a brunette, and Barbi Benton, my major romantic relationship of the early 1970s, was a brunette. But since the end of my marriage, all of my girlfriends have been blonds.

Hugh Hefner

I'm always told that what I say is controversial. Why is it controversial? Because I speak from a tradition that has now fallen out of favor with the dominant media in this country. And so when I say things like marriage should be between one man and one woman, I'm called a bigot.

Rick Santorum

Same-sex marriage would eliminate entirely in law the basic idea of a mother and a father for every child. It would create a society which deliberately chooses to deprive a child of either a mother or a father.

Keith O'Brien

I always felt that a marriage works best at a farm... where you're together and everybody has clear-cut roles; they have chores, 'you take care of this' and you know. But it's hard.

Ethan Hawke

My parents were, had a marriage of passion, and the passion was about their religious beliefs. They were both immigrant families that - well, my father's family came as Puritans to Massachusetts.

Phil Jackson

I've actually always wanted to write like a one-person show that was sort of a romantic comedy - a show that was kind of cynical about romance and marriage but ultimately embraced it. Because I feel like comedy is always cynical, inherently, because it's contrarian.

Mike Birbiglia

Whatever's missing in your relationship, including a marriage, is what you're not bringing to it.

Nadine Velazquez

And in a marriage you can't TRY and be married. You're married or you're not married... as far as I'm concerned.

Ringo Starr

I was very influenced by the musicals and romantic comedies of the 1930s. I admired Gene Harlow and such, which probably explains why, since the end of my marriage, I've dated nothing but a succession of blondes.

Hugh Hefner

Marriage ain't easy, but it's great most of the time.

Sean Penn

To be honest, marriage doesn't scare me and that, it's just once you've been together for so long, if you haven't got any kids it's just a big expensive day out for everyone else to enjoy, isn't it?

Karl Pilkington

The great secret of a successful marriage is to treat all disasters as incidents and none of the incidents as disasters.

Harold Nicolson

Dick Armey is an economic conservative. He is not a social conservative. He doesn't like to talk about marriage and about the unborn child, the sanctity of life and things like that. He wants to talk about smaller government.

James Dobson

Here's why I cannot vote for Rudy Giuliani. He's pro-abortion. He's never repudiated gay marriage in New York City or at least the civil unions in New York City. He's called a champion of gay rights. Rudy is opposed to school choice. He's in favor of open borders.

James Dobson

Homosexuals can be, you know, committed to each other. And they have freedom to behave in the ways that they do, but they cannot be a family. They cannot be married. I mean, virtually every culture in the history of the world has considered marriage to be between one woman and one man.

James Dobson

I've always been the kind of person that if I take on anything professionally it means commitment to me, so you take it on if you can commit to it and if you know you can accommodate and give your best to it and that's what you do, and I have always done that throughout my life - before marriage, after marriage, before motherhood, after motherhood.

Aishwarya Rai Bachchan

I don't think I will go for an arranged marriage, but I am not against arranged marriages.

Ranbir Kapoor

We all have a childhood dream that when there is love, everything goes like silk, but the reality is that marriage requires a lot of compromise.

Raquel Welch

Gay marriage is the last bastion of, to me... as a legal, ceremonial, sentimental and religious side, it's one of the last steps. Retaining your job being one of the earlier steps, like, not getting kicked out of your job because you're gay.

Gus Van Sant

Well, my view before was a Western view, and I certainly understand marriage equality and civil rights, equal rights for all, but having visited developing nations and some of the poorest nations in the world, I realize how deep it goes and how much work really needs to be done to create equality for all.

Jason Mraz

Everyone saw me on TV or read articles, and it was all about my great marriage, the white picket fence, all this success and my perfect life. But behind the scenes, it was a struggle.

Lindsey Vonn

A song like 'Once in a Lifetime' is inspired by my marriage - it's a good, life-changing happening in my life. I think when you find your once-in-a-lifetime love, that's what everybody's looking for.

Keith Urban

One hopes, of course, that a relationship grows and becomes a deep and wonderful marriage and friendship that lasts forever. But that's not always the case.

Alana Stewart

Marriage is like a bank account. You put it in, you take it out, you lose interest.

Irwin Corey

The great thing about marriage is that it creates trust, the most precious of things.

Theodore Zeldin

I would like to thank those who spoke boldly against the 'gay marriage float' in the 2014 Rose Parade. Apparently, that vigorous opposition came from perhaps millions of people, and it had a significant influence on how the matter was handled on network and cable television.

James Dobson

I think that with marriages, people have to understand that you have to look at your marriage and understand what is needed in your marriage - not what people think your marriage should be or what people want your marriage to be.

Jada Pinkett Smith

Marriage commissioners who choose not to marry homosexuals are being fired. A Knights of Columbus chapter in British Columbia is in court because it chooses not allow a lesbian group to use its facility for marriage ceremonies. The list goes on.

Stockwell Day

Marriage may often be a stormy lake, but celibacy is almost always a muddy horse pond.

Thomas Love Peacock

Whatever the long-term legal prospects for same-sex marriage, President Obama's willingness to put the matter front and center in an election year can at least make him a candidate for inclusion in Kennedy's Profiles in Courage.

Robert Dallek

I suffered, I really suffered, with all three of my husbands. And I tried damn hard with all three, starting each marriage certain that it was going to last until the end of my life. Yet none of them lasted more than a year or two.

Ava Gardner

A miracle... my biggest accomplishment is my marriage so far. Because it's hard, everyone knows it's hard.

Gwen Stefani

I think it's unfortunate that there exists only one path in America to complete social legitimacy, and that is marriage. I think, for instance, that it would be far easier for Americans to elect a black president or a female president than an unmarried president.

Elizabeth Gilbert

Marriage is the most obvious public practice about which information is readily available. When combined with the traditional Jewish concern for continuity and self-preservation - itself only intensified by the memory of the Holocaust - marriage becomes the sine qua non of social membership in the modern Orthodox community.

Noah Feldman

My parents did not have a perfect marriage. It was pretty good, but it was not perfect. My marriage is not perfect. My wife is, but I happen to be imperfect. However, that does not discount the fact that the definition of marriage must be defended and protected.

Stockwell Day

My parents have a wonderful marriage, but they have been

together since my mother was 12, married when they were just teenagers and are barely ever separated. They even work together. As a result, I have always thought of marriage as involving the loss of a certain amount of autonomy.

Jessica Valenti

I have close family members as well as lots of close friends who are gay. Many of them strongly support gay marriage.

Tony Abbott

Women today have more of an overview of their lives and how marriage is or is not a part of it.

Helen Reddy

I'm for gay marriage, because I'm for gay divorce.

Melissa Etheridge

Marriage, in life, is like a duel in the midst of a battle.

Edmond About

Why did mainstream America come to accept marriage equality? Gay leaders had made a convincing case that gay families were like straight families and should have the same rights. The American spirit of fair play had been invoked.

Edmund White

My worldview, my philosophy, my attitudes, my relationships, my parenting, my marriage - everything has been transformed by my relationship with Christ.

Lee Strobel

In December 1998, I considered myself an expert on love. I was almost a year into a relationship, one that had grown more slowly than I had wished, but once it flowered it was much more stimulating than any marriage or relationship I had known.

Jane Smiley

I was raised Catholic. Not just a little bit Catholic, like my wife, Catherine. When she was young, many Catholics in France already barely went to church, except for the big three: baptism, marriage, and funeral. And only the middle one was by choice.

Frans de Waal

In articulating all my feelings about marriage equality, I almost don't know where to begin. And perhaps that's part of the problem. Why do we have to explain ourselves when it comes to issues of fairness and equality? Why is common sense not enough?

Scott Fujita

Mr. Speaker, I rise today in support of the definition of a marriage as between one man and one woman.

Randy Neugebauer

I am drawn to the mystery of marriage. You can never know what the contract is between two people, and that is a very strong subject. I think it may be my subject.

Mike Nichols

I was looking very much for a career. My second marriage to Stan Herman had ended, and I wanted very much to be independent, not take alimony from him, be on my own, do the right thing.

Linda Evans

I remember driving home one evening while they were reviewing the papers on the radio. One of the articles was about me separating from my wife. It's a weird thing to listen to a news report about the break-up of your marriage.

Rory Bremner

It's not a failure if a marriage or partnership ends after a certain number of years. I think, in general, we expect too much of partners. We can't fulfil a person's every single need and, after ten years or so, many relationships wear out. If we were more philosophical about it, we wouldn't try to blame the other person or be bitter.

Deborah Moggach

I suffered from a mild case of postpartum depression after my second child and the physical challenge of maintaining an overnight shift at CBS, a marriage, and two in diapers made the symptoms worse and everyone in the house paid the price.

Mika Brzezinski

I haven't been faithful to my wife. Our marriage has been tainted with my infidelities. I was irresponsible.

David Boreanaz

A lot of people seem to want to make the institution of marriage substitute for a real relationship.

Susan Faludi

In marriage, it's always that give and take and rebalancing that we have to do in how we can help each other. But, I have been known at times by my sons, that is the name that they call me-the Mitt stabilizer.

Ann Romney

My marriage was breaking up, and my marriage with Chong was breaking up. I had to come back and kind of start on my own again.

Cheech Marin

The rarity is the sudden epiphany or single turning point showing you with dramatic clarity that your marriage is over, although that does happen. Most relationships hover on a precipice for years before one party or the other finally decides it is time to jump, and coming to the decision isn't easy.

Laura Wasser

While I am impulsive in many areas of my life, marriage is not one of them.

Neil Strauss

The woman who has her being in marriage and motherhood has become part of antithetical reality, revoking property from the woman who remains in a condition of intangible femininity.

Rachel Cusk

This is a good time to ask apologists for the Islamic regime, who degrades Islam? Who imposes stoning, forced marriage of underage girls and flogging for not wearing the veil? Do such practices represent Iran's ancient history and culture, its ethnic and religious diversity? Its centuries of sensual and subversive poetry?

Azar Nafisi

The state's interest in marriage is stability. Generally speaking, polygamy does not work for stability. Inherent in the whole polygamous movement is a deep and abiding misogyny and denigration of women. So polygamy is objectionable on lots of grounds.

Gene Robinson

My first marriage was totally unsuitable and shouldn't have happened. It was a whirlwind, rebound thing. I was 23 or 24 - a baby.

Carol Vorderman

It's risky in a marriage for a man to come home too late, but it can sometimes pose an even greater risk if he comes home too early.

Marcel Achard

A marriage is a solemn affair. The tempest of emotions and the myriad of arrangements are giddying, and when one is faced with these, clothing seems to be the last of one's priorities.

Daphne Guinness

It's funny - I read that women look to chiseled-faced guys for one-night stands, and to round-faced guys for marriage. When I'm rounder in the face, I like to say, 'This is my long-term look.' Or 'This is my wife-and-kids look right here.'

Garrett Hedlund

I think that marriage is an amazing institution and should

be preserved, and you can have great marriages, and you must because sharing your life with someone is like the greatest thing. And I loved being able to set a good example for that on television.

Jenna Elfman

I'm extremely fascinated by marriage. I want to study marriage. I want to learn about it. I want to know it. I want to figure out whether or not I want to do it. I'm not just going to leap into it, because that's not good for anybody.

Adam Levine

Marriage, if one will face the truth, is an evil, but a necessary evil.

Menander

Either marriage is a destiny, I believe, or there is no sense in it at all, it's a piece of humbug.

Max Frisch

Gay marriage has jumped out of the closet on to the front page. Everyone from the president of the U.S. to retired four-star general Colin Powell is embracing the issue, now supported by most Americans. Still, a few people, like former First Lady Laura Bush appear to be conflicted.

Kitty Kelley

Twitter is the marriage of full-tilt narcissism and full-tilt voyeurism that has finally collided in 140 words.

Adam Goldberg

There may be people in my audience who may not agree with me on some particular issue - you know, say, as a gun owner, they may not agree with me, or, you know, someone may not agree with me on a gay marriage topic. Any of those things. But those shouldn't be the reasons you listen to my music.

Brad Paisley

I just read 'The Seven Principles for Making Marriage Work.' To be married 25 years, you have to put as much energy as I put into being an actor or being a great football player into being a better husband and a better father.

Terry Crews

Kim Kardashian's marriage to Kris Humphries famously lasted 72 days, and was reported in the tabloids as being all about the big bucks paid by magazines for the bridal photos: it is a spectacle of a bride-to-be as entrepreneur, not as romantic heroine; the groom, in this scenario, is nothing but a prop.

Naomi Wolf

I was a happy person before marriage. I'm definitely happier after marriage.

Vidya Balan

It was the only ambition I ever had - not to be a dancer or Hollywood movie star, but to be a housewife in a good marriage.

Doris Day

Well, my personal mission statement is that we want marriage equality in all 50 states. We want it not to be a state-by-state issue. We don't want it to be something the majority is voting on. I don't think the civil rights of any minority should be in the hands of any majority.

Jesse Tyler Ferguson

Every three or four shows, we have somebody that will come up onstage and propose marriage.

John Tesh

In a marriage, in any long-term relationship, not to bother with lying. There's no time for that. If you have any sort of secret life, it will come back to haunt you.

Andy Garcia

Marriage was never a dream or an ambition for me. I thank my real mother for the fact that - unlike my sitcom mother - she never put any pressure on me or my sister to marry.

Miranda Hart

I was glad to hear of that determination as I detest the practice of cousins marrying or any marriage between persons in which there can be traced the most distant relationship. I go for the improvement instead of the deterioration of our race.

Ezra Cornell

I believe in the institution of marriage. Of course being a Mormon, we believe in eternity rather than just till death do us part. If you really try hard, if you make it work, it's blissful. But I also know a marriage that isn't working can be painful.

Donny Osmond

If someone talks about union, fidelity, a monogamous
relationship, love, blessing; I would say it sounds like
marriage to me. And blessing, you see, I think is
undermining our sacrament of marriage.

George Carey

No Congress ever has seen fit to amend the Constitution to
address any issue related to marriage. No Constitutional
Amendment was needed to ban polygamy or bigamy, nor
was a Constitutional Amendment needed to set a uniform
age of majority to ban child marriages.

Judy Biggert

I did not have a personal relationship with Jesus until I met
my nanny, who helped me through a failing marriage and
raising my two boys in a New York City apartment. She
showed me by example what it was like to be able to talk
to Jesus and bring all my cares and worries to Him. That
was in 1990.

Kim Alexis

A good businessman never makes a contract unless he's
sure he can carry it through, yet every fool on earth is

perfectly willing to sign a marriage contract without considering whether he can live up to it or not.

Dalton Trumbo

I've praised Obama's record on same-sex equality as enthusiastically as anyone: it's one area where his record has been impressive. I understand, and have expressed, the emotional importance for LGBT Americans of his marriage announcement as well as its political significance.

Glenn Greenwald

In response to our fast-food culture, a 'slow food' movement appeared. Out of hurried parenthood, a move toward slow parenting could be growing. With vital government supports for state-of-the-art public child care and paid parental leave, maybe we would be ready to try slow love and marriage.

Arlie Russell Hochschild

Sleeping together is a euphemism for people, but tantamount to marriage with cats.

Marge Piercy

Although my marriage left me with three beautiful children, it also left me with a healthy dose of self-doubt, low self-esteem, and an extreme desire to be loved again. I was operating on empty, expecting to be paid in full.

Niecy Nash

Marriage is like a formality for me.

David Copperfield

I myself got married at a very young age. It has always intrigued me because marriage is very synthetic in an otherwise natural world.

Imtiaz Ali

I am very old-fashioned about marriage. It is for life and I mean it. I always knew that when I met the right girl, the life I had before - being single, in a band, girls everywhere - would be over.

Gary Numan

Studies have consistently shown that financial hardship is the biggest obstacle to heterosexual marriage, yet the Republican leadership has done precious little to help address the financial hardship faced by American families.

Kendrick Meek

At my core, what I think we need to do is to get the basics right again. We need to rebuild our family structure, stay away from redefining marriage, and stand by marriage as a union between a man and a woman.

Sam Brownback

For a few thousand years, women had no history. Marriage was our calling, and meekness our virtue. Over the last century, in stuttering succession, we have gained a voice, a vote, a room, a playing field of our own. Decorously or defiantly, we now approach what surely qualifies as the final frontier.

Stacy Schiff

There is a real sense of anger among many people who are married that the government, any government, thinks it has the ability to change the definition of an institution like marriage.

Philip Hammond

I have been doing marriage counseling for about 15 years and I realized that what makes one person feel loved, doesn't make another person feel loved.

Gary Chapman

The weaker partner in a marriage is the one who loves the most.

Eleonora Duse

In a sacred ground like marriage, you find yourself out of it at certain times for reasons unknown that can be destructive. There could be a demon that kind of comes out and overtakes you.

David Boreanaz

People used to say my son looked like a Mexican Biggie. And when he was first born, memories of Biggie... you know, we didn't always have the greatest days. For at least half the length of our marriage we were separated, so everyday was definitely not a good day.

Faith Evans

The definition of marriage cannot be disputed. It's right there in black and white and it's been the same since the start of Wikipedia.

Jesse Tyler Ferguson

My life, in some ways, has been a half-measure. I didn't commit myself all the way to my marriage and family, because I would have given up more. And I didn't go all the way with just being completely selfish. I always wonder where my career would be if I was more selfish.

Alec Baldwin

My parents had an arranged marriage, as did so many other people when I was growing up. My father came and had a life in the United States one way and my mother had a different one, and I was very aware of those things. I continue to wonder about it, and I will continue to write about it.

Jhumpa Lahiri

I invented the psychological histories and the relationship between Jack and Susan Stanton. I didn't know anything about the Clintons. I don't know more about the Clintons' marriage than you do.

Joe Klein

The principle of plural marriage was revealed to the Mormons amid much secrecy. Dark clouds hovered over the church in the early 1840s, after rumors spread that its founder, Joseph Smith, had taken up the practice of polygamy. While denying the charge in public, by 1843 Smith had shared a revelation with his closest disciples.

Scott Anderson

My marriage to my husband, Bart Conner in 1996 is my proudest personal moment.

Nadia Comaneci

If we did not look to marriage as the principal source of happiness, fewer marriages would end in tears.

Anthony Storr

Good production is like a beautiful marriage. It makes a happy home.

Timbaland

The whole Haley-Nathan marriage deal was a pretty good twist huh? I hope we got all of you with it. That particular story line even suprised me when I read it, it's a good one and it'll provide for some good stories to come.

James Lafferty

I love marriage. I think it's a wonderful institution and it's the most important decision you make.

Isla Fisher

I used to have a theory actually that, if you've had a good childhood, a good marriage and a little bit of money in the bank, you're going to make a lousy comedian.

David Steinberg

The ideal mother, like the ideal marriage, is a fiction.

Milton Sapirstein

To seduce a woman famous for strict morals, religious fervor and the happiness of her marriage: what could possibly be more prestigious?

Christopher Hampton

I am not married yet, but I think ultimately in a good marriage it is the relationship which is the most important thing. It is not a matter of who is right and who is wrong; it is a one plus one equals more than two.

Lawrence Bender

Opera is the original marriage of words and music, and there's a theatre element, a dramatic element. It's right up my alley.

Shane Koyczan

Marriage is sacred and protected and has nothing to do with violating our civil rights.

Jack Kingston

It's nice to be able to work; I'd love to be able to do another TV show I could do in Chicago so I could live and work in the same place. It's hard being a parent and being in a good marriage, and it all takes a lot of work, but if you're not there you can't do any of it.

Joan Cusack

I had a realization in the midst of my happy marriage that I had kind of lost most of my friends - my male friends in particular. And I started wondering if my wife, who was certainly my best friend, supplanted those relationships.

Matthew Weiner

Montanans believe in the right to make a good life for their families. How they define a family should be their business and their business alone. I'm proud to support marriage equality because no one should be able to tell a Montanan or any American who they can love and who they can marry.

Jon Tester

President Bush has a record of cutting taxes, has provided a prescription drug benefit for seniors, has upheld the Second Amendment and remains committed to stopping liberal activists judges who are redefining marriage.

Bill Shuster

Marriage, like death, is a debt we owe to nature.

Julia Ward Howe

My father was on the faculty in the Chemistry Department of Harvard University; my mother had one year of graduate work in physics before her marriage.

Kenneth G. Wilson

When the first fossils began to be found in eastern Africa, in the late 1950s, I thought, what a wonderful marriage this was, biology and anthropology. I was around 16 years old when I made this particular choice of academic pursuit.

Donald Johanson

I've heard that we come on earth in pairs, get separated only to meet once again through marriage. So whoever is there on this earth for me will eventually get paired with me. Till then, I'll enjoy my singlehood.

Rani Mukerji

Content and technology are strange bed fellows. We are joined together. Sometimes we misunderstand each other. But isn't that after all the definition of marriage?

Howard Stringer

Marriage, as an institution, is as dead as the dodo bird.

Joan Fontaine

You never go into a marriage expecting to get divorced. You go into a marriage expecting it's going to last forever, and you have a lot of ways you dream about the future. You have all these expectations, and then you have to adjust those expectations, and it can be a very unnerving, confusing time.

Jenna Fischer

There is no greater excitement than to support an intellectual wife and have her support you. Marriage is a partnership in which each inspires the other, and brings fruition to both of you.

Millicent Carey McIntosh

Culture and tradition have to change little by little. So 'new' means a little twist, a marriage of Japanese technique with French ingredients. My technique. Indian food, Korean food; I put Italian mozzarella cheese with sashimi. I don't think 'new new new.' I'm not a genius. A little twist.

Masaharu Morimoto

No Government has the moral authority to dismantle the universally understood meaning of marriage.

Keith O'Brien

Public-opinion polls show that Americans split about evenly on civil unions. But when the words 'gay marriage' are presented, they break 3-to-1 against it.

Dick Morris

I think that every state in the union should recognize same-sex marriage.

Cass Sunstein

I've done an informal, anecdotal survey about marriage, and I've found no evidence that it brings happiness.

Mary McCormack

There are powerful emotions that bring two people together in wonderful harmony in a marriage. Satan knows this, and would tempt you to try these emotions outside of marriage. Do not stir emotions meant to be used only in marriage.

Richard G. Scott

I had a happy marriage and a nice wife. I accomplished everything you can. What more can you want?

Max Schmeling

I do not think the gay population has been all that rabid for gay marriage. Note that I do not use the words 'gay community.' Expunge that expression from your vocabulary. We are not a community.

Larry Kramer

I've never understood what the upside of marriage would be for me personally.

Arsenio Hall

I don't care how handsome or fabulous or funny the groom is, or how sweet and accommodating the bride, or vice versa. Marriage is hard.

Jenna McCarthy

I would like it to be known that I have decided not to marry Group Capt. Peter Townsend. Mindful of the church's teaching that Christian marriage is indissoluble, and conscious of my duty to the Commonwealth, I have resolved to put these considerations before any others.

Princess Margaret

Whether it's mending a failing company, fighting corruption, tackling disease, or rebuilding a marriage, the hardest problems defy just-add-water remedies. Indeed, slapping on a Band-Aid when surgery is needed usually just makes things worse.

Carl Honore

Conventional wisdom tells us we'll only be happier after a divorce if the marriage itself was a war zone.

Ariel Gore

I was a Christian. I didn't want to have sex before marriage, I was a bit uptight and not very self-confident. I was a virgin until I was 26.

Jimmy Carr

They make Spy Kids, they make Scream, they make A Scary Movie. This doesn't do that, so it could be a very bad marriage. I'm trying to keep this potential nightmare quiet because we're just finishing editing.

Terry Gilliam

Conversations about money certainly are not sexy, but they should give each of you some clarity and enable you to enter into your marriage with a better understanding of each other and what is important. Work and home responsibilities, joint or separate accounts, budgets, etc. are all subjects which should be discussed.

Laura Wasser

I don't know that human beings were meant to mate for life or be monogamous. But, for me, the aspect of marriage that is troubling is that it's a contract that is governed by the state, and I don't want the state to have control over my personal affairs.

Laura Wasser

Maintaining marriage seems to be tougher than fatherhood: apparently it's the most difficult thing in the world.

Kelly Slater

Marriage is a definite no-no. I am totally married to my company. Emotionally, my mother fills up the void in my life. So there it is. My company is a spouse I will never cheat on, and my mother completes me as a son. I think I have a full family unit of my own.

Karan Johar

If the rights of civil partners are met differently in law to those of married couples, there is no discrimination in law, and if civil partnerships are seen as somehow 'second class' that is a social attitude which will change and cannot, in any case, be turned around by redefining the law of marriage.

John Sentamu

In a hundred years, Christianity will have mutated into something utterly unpredictable which, nevertheless, we'd recognize immediately. And same-sex marriage will be one of the fine old God-given traditions that conservatives leap to defend.

Francis Spufford

I'm not cynical about marriage or romance. I enjoyed being married. And although being single was fun for a while, there was always the risk of dating someone who'd owned a lunch box with my picture on it.

Shaun Cassidy

I never thought my marriage could be stronger, or I could be closer to Bill. We prayed on our own, but now we prayed together and you'll never know how much that means until you do it.

Giuliana Rancic

I am the most well-adjusted human being I know. I started out this investigation as a very happy man with a great career. I've got the life people dream about: I am rich, I am famous, I've got a fabulous marriage to an absolutely, spell-bindingly brilliant woman.

James Ellroy

I am the first one to go to university in my family. I am the first writer as well. My dad is a retired policeman, and my mom works for a glass-processing company. She is health-and-safety manager, and my stepfather is a plumber. I have four half siblings, one from my mom's marriage and three from my dad's marriage, so we are kind of scattered.

Samantha Shannon

The United States Supreme Court has repeatedly held that marriage is one of the most fundamental rights that we have as Americans under our Constitution.

Ted Olson

I rise today in support of Bill C-38, the Civil Marriage Act. I rise in support of a Canada in which liberties are safeguarded, rights are protected and the people of this land are treated as equals under the law.

Paul Martin

It was very difficult when I was trying to figure out how to have a marriage and babies and do this at the same time. There was no handbook. You were making it up as you went along.

Pat Benatar

I think there is a generation gap. I personally look forward to, as our generation becomes the leaders, you are gonna see a change, and I think hopefully gay marriage will be a part of that country.

Vanessa Kerry

I've learned this is a very long marriage doing a television show. I like the people that I work with to be people I enjoy, so you want to cast people who are as excited and enthusiastic as you are.

Shonda Rhimes

If you look at issues like immigration, gay marriage, gun regulation - these are all things that probably wouldn't be a source of much discussion at all in D.C., if they weren't sources of self-perpetuation.

Mark Leibovich

I think that's one of the most difficult things in any marriage - in order to build anything, you must be together. You can't build anything over the telephone.

Julie London

It is sad that the Republican leadership is not as interested as they say they are in protecting the institution of marriage as they are in waging a campaign to divide and distract the American people from the real issues that need to be addressed.

Kendrick Meek

The reality of marriage as the union of a mother and a father is grounded in our very biology.

Salvatore J. Cordileone

For women of my generation, it was the 'juggling act.' Jobs, marriage, children, homes, and aging parents were the balls we added, tossing them in the air as our lives filled up and praying they wouldn't come crashing down on our heads.

Willow Bay

For a while I didn't believe in marriage. But I think I do believe in having a love. I'm not saying only one love ever, but in having a good, solid relationship. I think that's possible.

Penn Badgley

Marriage always demands the greatest understanding of the art of insincerity possible between two human beings.

Vicki Baum

My characters always start well in movies. Almost every movie I've done starts with a happy marriage, it's all beautiful, wealthy, whatever... and then of course my husband leaves me, and everything falls apart.

Carole Bouquet

Would we be a better society if we made marriage simply a private contract between two individuals, with no wider implications of kinship and family? I do not believe that we would.

John Sentamu

I liked the premise of this material. I love the marriage relationship. They kind of keep each other honest, and they enjoy each other's sense of humor. Kind of a sexy but boring relationship.

Patricia Arquette

Today the House has a chance to give 25 million married couples the best Valentine's Day gift possible, elimination from the most unfair of taxes, the marriage tax penalty.

Jerry Weller

The whole institution of marriage itself really has no place in a progressive society.

Doug Stanhope

I don't want to make any judgments, and I don't want to preach, but I'm hoping that marriage can work: that when people do fall in love, when people do find their soul mate, everyone sticks to it. It has the potential to be a very powerful thing, marriage.

Jonathan Silverman

That's my prescription for a happy marriage - marry someone who doesn't do anything similar to what you do.

Maxine Kumin

Michael and I had great role models. Though his father has passed away, his parents had an amazingly strong marriage, as do mine. Both weathered really tough times. For us it has been normal to stay together through difficulties. We grew up witnessing that firsthand.

Tracy Pollan

The fact is, I am in my third marriage and I do not believe in divorce. But I was half the problem, I guarantee you. More than half the problem. I couldn't negotiate with the other women.

James Brolin

I call myself taking control of a situation, but sometimes you really have to learn to humble yourself and to submit yourself. I'm not really good with submission, so that's the part of marriage and relationships that I've found very hard to deal with.

Tichina Arnold

Never again! I can see no reason for marriage - ever at all. I've had it. Three times is enough.

Ingrid Bergman

I have to be asked, I guess, but I love the idea of marriage. I think it's beautiful. I'm such a romantic, and I always have been.

Portia de Rossi

Marriage! Nothing else demands so much of a man.

Henrik Ibsen

I prepare myself for rehearsals like I would for marriage.

Maria Callas

What I increasingly felt, in marriage and in motherhood, was that to live as a woman and to live as a feminist were two different and possibly irreconcilable things.

Rachel Cusk

Civil union is less than marriage. Marriage is a sacred and valued institution and ought to be afforded equal protection.

James McGreevey

People try much less hard to make a marriage work than they used to fifty years ago. Divorce is easier.

Mary Wesley

It's so important to keep a marriage alive with small treats and doing little things for each other. Just remembering to say nice things and to have listening time is vital. That ghastly phrase 'quality time' means taking three minutes to sit down and be still with someone rather than yelling over your shoulder as you rush out.

Joanna Lumley

Marriage was all a woman's idea and for man's acceptance of the pretty yoke, it becomes us to be grateful.

Phyllis McGinley

My parents had a great marriage. Interestingly, it made it harder for me in relationships because I knew what a good relationship looked like.

Candace Bushnell

Every society in the history of man has upheld the institution of marriage as a bond between a man and a woman. Why? Because society is based on one thing: that society is based on the future of the society. And that's what? Children. Monogamous relationships.

Rick Santorum

I would love to get married, first of all, from my children's perspective. People don't think of children when they think of gay marriage, but I do have children, and for them to see their family validated as other families are validated and protected by our government, yes.

Judy Gold

That is why I fought against abortion and that is why if I were still in the Senate I would be doing everything I could to defend the sanctity of marriage.

Jesse Helms

I worked with John, but I had enough sense to walk just a little ways behind him. I could have made more records, but I wanted to have a marriage.

June Carter Cash

The old welfare system was hurting people by discouraging work and marriage. Welfare reform, and now this legislation, will build on the understanding that work and strong families are the foundation upon which we build our future.

Jim Talent

Marriage equality is coming, and not merely to a theater near you.

Suzanne Brockmann

Marriage is one long conversation, chequered by disputes.

Robert Louis Stevenson

I believe the home and marriage is the foundation of our society and must be protected.

Billy Graham

We want our marriage to be a triumph, not a tragedy.

Joyce Meyer

Not cohabitation but consensus constitutes marriage.

Marcus Tullius Cicero

Marriage can be a magnificent lesson in becoming our best selves; that is true.

Marianne Williamson

Marriage, like everything else in the world, is holy or unholy depending on the purpose the mind ascribes to it.

Marianne Williamson

A man's friendships are, like his will, invalidated by marriage - but they are also no less invalidated by the marriage of his friends.

Samuel Butler

Books and marriage go ill together.

Moliere

After marriage, a woman's sight becomes so keen that she can see right through her husband without looking at him, and a man's so dull that he can look right through his wife without seeing her.

Helen Rowland

Culture, what you believe, what you value, how you live matters. Now, as fundamental as these principles are, they may become topics of democratic debates from time to time, so it is today with the enduring institution of marriage. Marriage is a relationship between a man and a woman.

Mitt Romney

I have not supported same-sex marriage. I have supported civil partnerships and contractual relationships.

Hillary Clinton

Every marriage is a mystery to me, even the one I'm in. So I'm no expert on it.

Hillary Clinton

I am against marriage, and I don't give a fig for society.

Brigitte Bardot

You don't really need to get married, but marriage is awfully nice. Everybody I know who got married, they say it really makes a difference. They feel very, very happy about it.

Lily Tomlin

My thoughts are that marriage is between a man and a

woman.

Benjamin Carson

The ceremony took six minutes. The marriage lasted about the same amount of time though we didn't get a divorce for almost a year.

Hedy Lamarr

A marriage contract to me is as binding as any in business, and I have always believed in sticking to an agreement.

J. Paul Getty

What is marriage, is marriage protection or religion, is marriage renunciation or abundance, is marriage a stepping-stone or an end. What is marriage.

Gertrude Stein

Society may no longer define marriage in the only way marriage has ever been defined in the annals of recorded history. Many societies allowed polygamy, many allowed child marriages, some allowed marriage within families; but none, in thousands of years, defined marriage as the union of people of the same sex.

Dennis Prager

When the rose and the cross are united the alchemical
marriage is complete and the drama ends. Then we wake
from history and enter eternity.

Robert Anton Wilson

Marriage is like twirling a baton, turning hand springs or
eating with chopsticks. It looks easy until you try it.

Helen Rowland

One doesn't have to get anywhere in a marriage. It's not a
public conveyance.

Iris Murdoch

I don't see any reason for marriage when there is divorce.

Catherine Deneuve

I've always been suspicious of TV, I've always found
music and video to be an unhappy marriage.

Keith Richards

When you are young, do not get involved in steady dating. When you reach an age where you think of marriage, then is the time to become so involved.

Gordon B. Hinckley

I think even in a good marriage, especially if you stay together long enough, there are going to be events that happen.

Tori Amos

I am oftentimes the ear for some people that I know and love. Which I like being. I don't know if I'd like being a marriage counselor, though, because that's too deep for me.

Jurnee Smollett

No persons professing to be Christians should enter the marriage relation until the matter has been carefully and prayerfully considered from an elevated standpoint, to see if God can be glorified by the union.

Ellen G. White

When you're unhappy in your marriage, your children are

the ones who suffer.

Christina Aguilera

I never believed marriage was a lasting institution. I thought that to be married for five years was to be married forever.

Lauren Bacall

I didn't want to be one of those women who wake up at 63 years old and realize they've missed the window of opportunity for marriage and children.

Alanis Morissette

I'm completely comfortable with gay marriage.

Elizabeth Edwards

Marriage is socialism among two people.

Barbara Ehrenreich

Take this marriage thing seriously - it has to last all the way to the divorce.

Roseanne Barr

Have you ever heard of a good marriage growing in front of the cameras?

Brigitte Bardot

Inspirations never go in for long engagements; they demand immediate marriage to action.

Brendan Behan

I do support a constitutional amendment on marriage between a man and a woman, but I would not be going into the states to overturn their state law.

Michele Bachmann

Marriage is like paying an endless visit in your worst clothes.

J. B. Priestley

I got a few marriage proposals in my 20s. I just wasn't ready. I just knew if I committed, I would've wound up doing something wrong, messing it up. I still felt like I had some living to do.

Queen Latifah

When someone comes up to me and says, 'Mary, you helped save my marriage', or, 'Mary, you helped me get out of this abusive relationship', I'm in it, really in their lives. And I'm so passionate about my feelings, but also about showing people the way through theirs.

Mary J. Blige

As marriage goes, I think most people sort of set being - you know getting married as the goal as opposed to being married.

Ashton Kutcher

I was raised on government cheese. As an adult, in my first marriage, my husband and I worked real hard just to go bankrupt. I happened to write some jokes about it. I did real well for myself.

Roseanne Barr

Let a man do what he will by a single woman, the world is encouragingly apt to think Marriage a sufficient amends.

Samuel Richardson

There are repercussions to everything, even advancement and success. And I think that the repercussions to my success was the loss of my marriage.

Jill Scott

TV does a thing that film can never do. It takes you to a place that no novel written after the late 19th century can. You can just go through people's lives; it's like a marriage.

Joss Whedon

I came to the United States because I fell in love, and I forced my guy - I forced him into marriage. And so I became a resident. And then I realized that I couldn't bring my children. I couldn't sponsor my children if I wasn't a citizen. So I became a citizen. But by then I had learned to love this country; I have received a lot from this country.

Isabel Allende

I have a lot of skepticism about marriage and monogamy.

Rashida Jones

You know, I believe that marriage is between a man and a

woman.

Carly Fiorina

We must have great respect for these people who also suffer and who want to find their own way of correct living. On the other hand, to create a legal form of a kind of homosexual marriage, in reality, does not help these people.

Pope Benedict XVI

I am a fan of marriage and a fan of being committed to the right person.

Joan Collins

It devastates me now that I have been reduced to a Hollywood statistic - another joke marriage.

Sophia Bush

It's not someone else's responsibility to honor my marriage. It's my responsibility.

David Duchovny

I can't imagine having a real personal thing, like divorce and marriage, all those things, being in the public eye. I try to not talk about anything personal, and then nobody has the fire to throw back at you, like 'You said this back then!'

Kirsten Dunst

Marriage feels like an industry with catering and really expensive bands.

Rashida Jones

Coming to terms with the fact that my marriage was a failure was devastating and very difficult.

Sarah McLachlan

There are two basic restrictions on marriage in the Bible: Number one, she should marry a man. Number two, he should be a Christian.

John Piper

Isn't that the ultimate homeland security, standing up and defending marriage?

Rick Santorum

For me working on the marriage and not making the easy choice of cheating was something that I could not do.

Al Goldstein

Righteous marriage is a commandment and an essential step in the process of creating a loving family relationship that can be perpetuated beyond the grave.

David A. Bednar

Long-term relationships are an everyday choice. It's harder to be in a marriage than it is to bounce from one relationship to the next.

Pink

I'm in love with love and totally believe in marriage, but that's not even on my radar right now. I am not putting energy into dating.

Selena Gomez

I think you may see again a rise at the federal government level for a - a call for the federal constitutional amendment, because people want to make sure that this definition of marriage remains secure, because after all, the family is the fundamental unit of government.

Michele Bachmann

By divine design, men and women are intended to progress together toward perfection and a fulness of glory. Because of their distinctive temperaments and capacities, males and females each bring to a marriage relationship unique perspectives and experiences.

David A. Bednar

I was a bartender for a long time, so I know how to make drinks, but I'm more likely to offer them than to have them. I think this is one of the reasons why I get to live longer than my great-grandmother did, and why I get to produce more writing than she did, and why my marriage isn't in dire straits.

Elizabeth Gilbert

There was no religious ceremony connected with marriage among us, while on the other hand the relation between man and woman was regarded as in itself mysterious and holy.

Charles Eastman

If I go into a relationship with an artist, which at most is going to last five years, we have a 100-page contract covering every eventuality. Whereas with marriage you go into it with no contract, with laws that date back hundreds of years, and I don't think that's right.

Simon Cowell

A hundred years ago, if you had a child out of marriage, you'd be a social disgrace. Today women feel comfortable enough economically and culturally to bring up a child without a recognized commitment from a man.

Helen Fisher

If you look at Jack Benny, George Burns, or Don Rickles, they've all had long, successful marriages. So, I think there's something about laughter and the durability of a marriage.

Bob Newhart

You either believe marriage and human sexuality are sacred, or you do not.

Kirk Cameron

Marriage was never a destination with me.

Diane von Furstenberg

I always felt as though, 'If nothing else, I have a successful marriage.'

Willie Aames

Marriage made more sense when it was indissoluble. It's the woman trying to cope with the strains of a one-parent family who will suffer most from the relaxation of the divorce laws.

Germaine Greer

But I think it's up to a local congregation to determine whether or not a marriage should be blessed of God. And it shouldn't be up to the government.

Tony Campolo

President Bush once said that marriage is a sacred institution and should be reserved for the union of one man and one woman. If this is the case - and most Americans would agree with him on this - then I have to ask: Why is the government at all involved in marrying people?

Tony Campolo

Marriage is a religious and state issue.

Jim DeMint

Same-sex marriage is not the future.

Maggie Gallagher

I've always been clear, I support the traditional definition of marriage.

Stephen Harper

Most of these alternative arrangements, so-called, arise out of the ruins of marriages, not as an improvement of old fashioned marriage.

Christopher Lasch

The Left despises Texas, with its stellar record of job growth; Texas, with its strong support for traditional marriage and the sanctity of life; Texas, the root of the conservative tree. Should the Left succeed in its attempt to turn Texas purple, America could turn permanently blue.

Ben Shapiro

I'm not eager to jump into marriage again. I'm in the corner right now, wearing my dunce cap. That area is obviously a nightmare.

Lisa Marie Presley

It's all kind of a big illusion: the white picket fence and the perfect marriage and the kids. Check that box off, check that box off, and move forward.

Sarah McLachlan

People should be allowed to marry, and gay marriage should be out there. If a man or a woman has a good partner and they love each other with their heart and soul, let them marry. I am very much for gay marriage.

Pierce Brosnan

Being in a successful marriage is no different than being cast in a successful movie. It's all about who you pick; in that first moment, did you pick the right person? I think you need to pick somebody who's more interested in being married than in getting married.

Rob Lowe

Well, you know, the definition of second marriage is the

triumph of hope over experience.

George Will

I'm an activist for gay marriage equality and children's rights. I'm the face of Share Our Strength.

Sandra Lee

Marriage is an ongoing thing, man. You continue to work at it. But it's joyful. And joyous. I don't care if people are living without a marriage certificate. It's just about people, in some way, saying to each other, 'I commit to you. I will help you in this life.'

James McAvoy

I've always had bizarre, negative feelings about anything traditional, like marriage and family. I never thought something like that worked.

Gerard Way

Marriage is gonna be your stability through everything.

Miranda Lambert

During my first marriage, my career was the most important thing in my life.

Michael Douglas

It took me too long to realise that if you go to a marriage counsellor to resolve problems, it's in his interest to keep the marriage going.

Michael Douglas

My marriage and my families come certainly before my career.

Michael Douglas

Marriage, at this point in my life? I'm not interested in it. Yet. Maybe later when I'm 35 or 40.

Amanda Seyfried

Marriage was defined by God a long time ago. Marriage is almost as old as dirt, and it was defined in the garden between Adam and Eve - one man, one woman for life till death do you part. So I would never attempt to try to redefine marriage. And I don't think anyone else should either.

Kirk Cameron

In 1977 we played America and Europe three times, and Japan - my marriage suffered as a result. My then wife took the kids to Canada to be near her parents.

Phil Collins

Clearly, if it is sensible to hold a referendum on independence, it is crucial that we have one on marriage. It is the only way the country can move forward on this issue. Let all those who have a view on this subject place their trust in the Scottish people and let Scotland decide.

Keith O'Brien

It is statistically proven that the strongest institution that guarantees procreation and continuity of the generations is marriage between one man and one woman. We don't want genocide. We don't want to destroy the sacred institution of marriage.

Alveda King

Men go into marriage with virtually no expectations whatsoever. Ten years later, the men are delightfully surprised to find out that it's actually kind of nice, and the women have sort of had to take a nose dive from what they thought it was going to be.

Elizabeth Gilbert

The rule with marriage is the less you talk about it the better, as far as I can tell.

Jennifer Garner

Marriage is the mother of the world. It preserves kingdoms, and fills cities and churches, and heaven itself.

Jeremy Taylor

I'd like to have a successful marriage, not for the sake of labelling or branding, but because I believe in the institution of marriage.

Sonam Kapoor

My marriage is incredibly important to me. It's the place from which I engage in the world every day, and the place to which I return every day.

Chelsea Clinton

I've had two terrific relationships, but both ended in

marriage.

Jane Seymour

I don't know what my version of a relationship or marriage is yet, because the typical model seems a little broken to me.

Michelle Williams

I'm all for same-sex marriage.

Tori Spelling

When your first marriage goes into tragedy, you become very battle-scarred... I even thought of suicide. Luckily, I had known some happy marriages.

Paul Engle

Above all, we must have great respect for these people who also suffer and who want to find their own way of correct living. On the other hand, to create a legal form of a kind of homosexual marriage, in reality, does not help these people.

Pope Benedict XVI

My grandparents got married at a very young age, and a lot of what I think about marriage is based on their relationship. I watched them over the years and saw how they dealt with everything together, as a team.

Kyle Chandler

For most of us, when our 'dreams' - I use the word with reservations - came true, and marriage and motherhood became a reality, the romcoms, like horoscopes, swiftly lost their allure.

Mariella Frostrup

I made an awful mess of my first marriage. It was hard to live with me being me. I was so abnormal. I mean, most writers struggle. I hadn't struggled. I couldn't suddenly go down to the PEN Club and behave like a normal human being, because most of those guys were struggling to make a couple of thousand pounds a year.

John le Carre

Marriage of attraction is a gamble anyway, so you might as well marry into a family that is similar to your own, and make that much less of an adjustment. But the 'love marriage', as it is called, is equally common in India now. But it would be interesting to do a comparison of what would work better. Marriage is hard work, and it is a gamble.

Mira Nair

You know what's funny? I don't ever feel the need to escape. I have a strong marriage. I like my life. You hear about these guys having midlife crises - I don't see that happening to me.

Harry Connick, Jr.

Marriage takes work - it doesn't just happen.

Lara Stone

I had a girlfriend when I was 17-18, and when she was 21, she wanted us to get married. I couldn't do that, because my game was my priority. We had to part ways, and there was no guilt because I had never committed to marriage.

Suresh Raina

The marriage didn't work out but the separation is great.

Liz Smith

The truth is you can have a great marriage, but there are

still no guarantees.

Demi Moore

I had a friend who, after 25 years of marriage, found himself trying to date again, and it was completely different. Everything had changed, and he had to reacquaint himself. It was funny even talking to him about it. For someone who has been out of the loop, it's a different world.

Steve Carell

Anything outside marriage seems like freedom and excitement.

Jeanette Winterson

I don't think having separate bathrooms is a key to a successful marriage, if you love one another.

Ewan McGregor

Marriage is a custom brought about by women who then proceed to live off men and destroy them, completely enveloping the man in a destructive cocoon or eating him away like a poisonous fungus on a tree.

Richard Harris

There's something about marriage that is not as intensely romantic or interesting as a couple's first meeting.

John Sandford

Spending only what the country can afford, rewarding savings, encouraging independence, supporting marriage: people know that these things are common sense.

William Hague

My parents separated when I was four. It wasn't the smoothest of divorces, but then as my mother always says, you can't have a passionate marriage without a passionate divorce.

Sophie Ellis-Bextor

People need jobs, people need happy and successful lives; there should be marriage between one man and one woman, there should the value of person from conception until natural death.

Alveda King

Marriage equality changed life for people.

Andrew Cuomo

The hypocrisy and false piety of the deniers aside, the relationships of gays have no effect on heteros. Especially all the heteros who've done such a marvelous job of debasing marriage on their own all these many years.

John Ridley

Marriage, laws, the police, armies and navies are the mark of human incompetence.

Dora Russell

Is marriage for ever? I think you get married with the intention that it will be, but who knows?

Courteney Cox

In the Hillary Clinton model, the wife chooses to support the straying husband while wearing a distressed and presumably pained expression in public. She stays in the marriage as a way to serve both her personal ambition as well as their shared ambition to achieve ever-greater positions of power and influence.

Monica Crowley

On both 'The Bachelor' and 'The Bachelorette,' it seems like proposing marriage is equivalent to saying, 'Let's date.' Everyone knows those aren't the same things.

Patti Stanger

Barack Obama's decision to come out in favour of gay marriage may be a historic occasion, but it is not an isolated one. His administration has been making pro-gay noises for some time; his demographic in the upcoming election is young and educated, precisely the group that favours equality for the LGBT community.

Edmund White

The culmination of a long struggle was 2013, which could clearly be labeled the Year of the Gay. State after state had legalized gay marriage, despite intense opposition from the religious right.

Edmund White

For the life of me, I don't understand what honest motive there is in putting this in front of this body to philosophically debate marriage on a constitutional amendment that is not going to happen, and which is enormously divisive in all of our communities.

Dianne Feinstein

If the court strikes down the Defense of Marriage Act, is that a 'liberal' result enabling gay couples married in states where gay marriage is legal to enjoy the same economic advantages that federal laws now grant to straight couples? Or is it a 'conservative' ruling, limiting the federal government's ability to override state power?

Jeff Greenfield

Most Americans don't care about gay marriage.

Dan Savage

I don't know if I'm built for marriage.

Jamie Foxx

I love marriage. I failed at marriage, but I'd rather go into anything with gusto and fail than go into it half-assed.

Kirstie Alley

I think marriage is ghastly.

Rupert Everett

When you're old-fashioned like I am, you know marriage
is forever. Those vows are a promise.

Brad Paisley

No marriage can stand up under the strain of incessant
association.

Johnny Weissmuller

Can you have a heritage more American than Obama's?
The literal marriage of the immigrant and native. Born in
our most diverse state. One without an ethnic majority, but
where people of mixed race make up some 20 percent of
the total population. There is nothing about Obama's
background that isn't truth to the tired saw of the American
melting pot.

John Ridley

'Smurfs' just seemed like a great way to represent a young
father to be, guy in a marriage, work in conflict, and I was
really interested in the technical CG side of things. I'd
never done a movie that I thought would be so physical
and yet so precise. So I was intrigued by all of that.

Neil Patrick Harris

I was just so lucky to have a wonderful life after a tough marriage.

Lynn Johnston

Sooner or later they are going to live in a New York City where gay marriage is not only legal, but it's common and they don't even notice.

Anthony Weiner

Marriage is an institution that existed before governments existed. It's something that reflects nature and reflects God and God's will for us. And both from the standpoint of faith and reason it makes all the sense in the world. And it's beneficial for society.

Rick Santorum

I would absolutely, definitely never sell my wedding pictures to a magazine. I'd like it to be a special day, not a photo shoot. And once you've done that, your marriage becomes everybody else's business.

Katherine Jenkins

Agreement is never reached in love. The life of a wife and husband who love each other is never at rest. Whether the marriage is true or false, the marriage portion is the same: elemental discord.

Jean Giraudoux

When David Arquette and I got engaged we started therapy together. I'd heard that the first year of marriage is the hardest, so we decided to work through all that stuff early.

Courteney Cox

Love is an obsessive delusion that is cured by marriage.

Phil Spector

Marriage requires searing honesty at all costs. I learned that from my third wife.

Alan Arkin

Growing up, my birthday was always Confederate Memorial Day. It helped to create this profound sense of awareness about the Civil War and the 100 years between the Civil War and the civil rights movement and my parents' then-illegal and interracial marriage.

Natasha Trethewey

There are times when marriage is not such a comfortable place... But you find your way; you become a different person. You grow into it. And you have to work at marriage every day.

Kajol

Well you know, I think a lot of us in marriage know that you play different roles at different times. And Mitt can get very intense, and I can have the ability to kind of talk him off the rails sometimes and say, 'Hey let's look at what is really important and let's do that now.'

Ann Romney

I am for gay marriage. Or same-sex marriage. I don't want to say it the wrong way. I think people are sensitive to it. I have been painted as being this right-wing zealot on choice. Nothing could be further from the truth.

Harold Ford, Jr.

I know that the odds are against a marriage lasting 60

years.

Darrell Royal

And that is why marriage and family law has emphasized the importance of marriage as the foundation of family, addressing the needs of children in the most positive way.

John Boehner

Marriage was probably the worst mistake I ever made in my life.

Tony Dorsett

Design, to me, is part psychology, part sociology, and part magic. A good decorator should know what's going on in someone's marriage and how their kids are doing in school.

Nate Berkus

A man's love, till it has been chastened and fastened by the feeling of duty which marriage brings with it, is instigated mainly by the difficulty of pursuit.

Anthony Trollope

I believe in the institution of marriage and it's like a tag to cement the relationship for your friends, family and public.

Kareena Kapoor Khan

I wanted my marriage to work, but it didn't.

Diane Abbott

Do the bishops seriously imagine that legalising gay marriage will result in thousands of parties to heterosexual marriages suddenly deciding to get divorced so they can marry a person of the same sex?

Malcolm Turnbull

Marriage can be expensive, and if I lose millions then it'll be the best millions I've spent.

Seth Rogen

I believe in marriage and fidelity.

Gloria Vanderbilt

I believe wholeheartedly in marriage. I don't exclusively mean a marriage with a legal contract, but any relationship that constitutes a marriage because of the quality of their relationship.

Helen Reddy

I don't think it's a great leap to go from civil unions to gay marriage - I may be in the minority in believing that.

Harold Ford, Jr.

While 45 of the 50 States have either a State constitutional amendment or a statute that preserves the current definition of marriage, left-wing activist judges and officials at the local levels have struck down State laws protecting marriage.

John Boehner

Even though my first marriage broke up, I'd say that I've had two good marriages and two good men. I've been very lucky. I like to think it's karma because, in a relationship, I give 300 per cent. I'm straight with my men, and I like to think it comes back.

Suzi Quatro

I am much more open to plural marriage than I was before, and I now support it in certain situations. I do believe it is right for some people. But our example in America today is gross abuse - I can't support it in fundamentalist compounds.

Ginnifer Goodwin

My second marriage had a lot to do with alcohol.

Mercedes McCambridge

I support gay marriage. I support gay marriage because I believe Conservatives support the institutions of commitment.

George Osborne

The only way marriage can work is if a man respects the woman and she is a thinking woman and he wants to work on the marriage.

Al Goldstein

I still believe in marriage.

Frank Bruno

My parents' marriage was very rocky. They were always

arguing. When they split up when I was in my 20s, my brother and I were both delighted because we knew they weren't good for each other.

Gail Porter

The defense of marriage is the defense of freedom. Neither of which is obsolete.

Nancy Pearcey

I was sent to a nice Church of England girls' school and at that time, after university, a woman was expected to become a teacher, a nurse or a missionary - prior to marriage.

Kate Adie

I hope gay marriage will be legal in every state.

Mark Consuelos

If love means never having to say you're sorry, then marriage means always having to say everything twice.

Estelle Getty

I don't want to go into a marriage just because of my age -
too many people make that mistake. But of course I'd like
to be married one day - I dream of having children because
I adore kids so, so much.

Shilpa Shetty

In all seriousness, I don't get people who need to make a
proposal a bigger deal than marriage already is.

Julie Klausner

I guess because the shows were activist in their own way -
the marriage of my public activism and my career
activism, you know - people understand me very well.
They also understand there's a very strong bipartisan part
in all of this.

Norman Lear

My marriage had been impulsive. That marriage should
have been short-lived instead of the 23 years it spanned.

Joseph Barbera

Out of control judicial activism threatens traditional
marriage in America.

Ernest Istook

Marriage cannot be severed from its cultural, religious and natural roots without weakening the good influence of society.

Jack Kingston

While I believe in marriage as an institution, I am also petrified of it.

Shahid Kapoor

The way that same-sex marriage should reach the federal level is that it absolutely should be decided by the Supreme Court as quickly as possible. It's a 14th Amendment issue. There's no argument about it.

Tony Kushner

My thinking is lot more different with many actresses in the industry. I don't understand why people in showbiz put their profession of acting in the back seat after marriage.

Kareena Kapoor Khan

They say that when a woman wants to end a relationship,

she cuts off all of her hair. I've done that twice in my marriage but am still married.

Leslie Mann

We are very puritan in America. We still hold true to these really antiquated values, this idea of the sanctity of marriage.

Zoe Lister-Jones

Marriage is a team effort. Both of us share that philosophy.

Nick Lachey

I do believe in soulmates and happy/successful marriages. No marriage can be happy 24x7 for 365 days. Both partners have to make the relationship work, is what I believe in.

Kajol

But I wanted marriage for myself. I was not calculating about it. I wish I was more calculating.

Linda McCartney

I think gay marriage should be the national law.

Rose McGowan

Success is hard in general for most women. We now have such busy lives, and we're told we can do everything - you know, we can have the relationship and the marriage and the kids and the career.

Cat Deeley

Men act out like they're horrified by marriage, but when they find the woman of their dreams, they love it.

Rachel Hunter

Marriage is the grave or tomb of wit.

Margaret Cavendish

Neither man nor woman is perfect or complete without the other. Thus, no marriage or family, no ward or stake is likely to reach its full potential until husbands and wives, mothers and fathers, men and women work together in unity of purpose, respecting and relying upon each other's strengths.

Sheri L. Dew

I have a very intense marriage.

James Ellroy

Only after I faced the unhappiness of my first marriage did I start on the path of personal growth.

Judith Wright

The Republicans find their faith imperiled by Barney Frank's marriage. There is always a shadow on the wall, a monster in the closet, a mysterious rustling in the teeming underbrush of the conservative Id.

Charlie Pierce

www.ingramcontent.com/pod-product-compliance
Lightning Source LLC
Chambersburg PA
CBHW070640290526
45790CB00001B/150